SERUM

A NOVEL

I0145907

CHRISTOPHER
MCDONALD

Serum

www.ChristopherMcDonald.com

ISBN: 978-0-9905341-3-6 (Hardcover)
ISBN: 987-0-9905341-4-3 (eBook)
ISBN: (Paperback)

Edited by: Victor Smiler & Sarah Anderson
Author Photograph: Emily Clay

Social Media
Facebook.com/author.christophermcdonald
@ChristopherPMcD

✠

First Edition Paperback
2017

Beyond the ideas of wrongdoing and right-doing there is a field. I will meet you there. ~Rumi

For my family

CHAPTER 1

SERUM

The crime scene was of gruesome sorts. There was blood and lots of it. For DR. Miller, she had seen many like this, and more than likely see many more. In a city like New York, this sort of thing happened all the time. Out of all the examiners she was the Chief Examiner. The one they called out when things were exceptionally bloody.

As she approached the crime scene tape, she passed by a crowd trying to get a glimpse of something. As she approached the yellow tape line, she was greeted by the detective in charge, William Cox.

"I hope you brought something to cover the shoes." He pointed down at her white stilettos.

"Always, Will, always..." She said. She took a pair of baby blue shoe covers from her purse. The covers basically looked like small hair nets.

Lacy Miller moved toward the two bodies lying in the alley way that connected two apartment buildings. She took out a pad and paper from her oversized mustard Hermes purse. "What happened to you?" she said to the first of two men as she leaned over the body.

Detective Cox watched as she circled the body not touching it. He has watched her take up to an hour before ever laying hands on the body. She moved like a vulture circling its prey. After taking notes on one, she moved to the other. After careful thought, she looked up and addressed Will. "You are looking for a knife about 6 inches long with a serrated edge and 22 caliber."

"Wow, you can just tell that by circling them like that?" Will asked.

"What can I say they speak to me," Dr. Miller replied with a smile. "There is a 3rd person involved here. He will have both the gun and the knife if he hasn't ditched them.

"Is there anything you need here before we finish processing?" William asked.

"No... Just make sure you take good blood samples from all of this. I would love to find DNA from a third person here." Dr. Miller took of her unused gloves and walked toward the tape line; she paused and looked back. "Once I get them to the lab I can make sure about the weapon. Tell my understudies not to mess with any of the wounds."

"Will do..." Detective Cox waved as she walked back under the tape line.

A patrol cop at the scene approached detective Cox and said, "Man that's one piece of ass. '

Detective Cox frowned at his unprofessionalism and said, "Man get back we have work to do."

Detective Cox and his colleges from the homicide division of the NYPD wrapped up the scene taking as many blood samples and photographing

SERUM

every angle. Dr. Miller's junior examiners and lab geeks then swooped in to take liver temps and bag the body to go to the lab.

Dr. Miller made it to the lab the next day with the two bodies lying side by side in her autopsy room. Her staff had taken the clothes off and had already started to run the test need. Dr. Miller again walked around the table circling.

Talking out loud to the two corpses, "What were you fighting over? Drugs? I will name you one, pointing at the corpus closest to the door. You had a gun. Number two brought a knife to a gun fight. Then there is number three that finished number one off before running. Both of you had no wallet or anything on you. I suspect number three wanted those too."

She moved to number two with gunshot wounds. There were three all were in the chest. She could see by the location of one it hit the aorta. He bleeds out in seconds. She moved to number one again. He had several defensive wounds on the underside of his hands. I bet the third guy has one or two as well. "Number two you started the fight. You didn't realize number one had a gun. Could this have been a mugging gone wrong?"

"Victim number one could not have been killed by victim number two. He has a deep knife wound in the breastplate. This would have taken someone

10

strong to plunge the knife in like that. Number two had been shot and was bleeding out and would not have the strength to do it. Number one could not have shot number two if he had just been stabbed in the chest."

"Who is number three and why was he there?" She said aloud circling the tables. "What was this all about? Talk to me damn it."

She continued to pace back and forth between the two tables. Thinking, pondering trying to find some information that would help the investigation. There was nothing that stuck in her craw more than not knowing what happened and why.

After she exhausted all of her deductive powers she prepared the corpuses for the autopsy. Everything from here was to be routine. Dr. Miller started with number one. This was only the natural order of things for her. She would then move on to number two. Taking full notations on every puncture or bullet hole.

No matter how hard they tried, and they did try, the murder of number one and number two would forever remain unsolved.

CHAPTER 2

CHRISTOPHER MCDONALD

Every Friday for lunch Lacy met with her college best friend for a long lunch. Mark was a lawyer and a damn good one. Lacy always told herself it was good to have a best friend as a lawyer. She never actually needed him until her divorce the prior year. No matter what the two were going through they always cleared their calendars for Friday lunches.

This particular Friday lunch was to be at Gusto's an Italian bistro. Mark and Corey arrived first. Corey was Mark's partner and had been for going on five years now. Lacy loved Corey as she did Mark, and accepted him as her family.

Lacy spotted the two sitting on the patio from down the street. Both sitting on one side of the table in their suits with matching pastel ties. They made eye contact and all exchanged a wave as she approached. She quickly moved through the crowd of tables on a busy Friday at lunch to take her seat across from her best friend and his partner

"I love the ties guys." She said while taking her seat and placing her incredible designer handbag next to her chair. She made sure to put one chair leg through the strap to avoid a grab and run while outside.

"Thanks," Corey replied. "The tie thing was my idea." He took a long sip of his water.

"How is work?" Mark asked her.

SERUM

"Guys you don't even want to know." She raised her hand as to let the waiter know she had arrived. "The last couple days have been horrible. A case is driving me bonkers."

Corey jumped in, "Is it the stabbing-shooting case? We just wrote a piece on that for the paper." Corey was a journalist for the Globe, a not so credible newspaper. "Do you have any inside information you can give me on the story. I would love to be able to be the one to break it." Mark pinched his leg from under the table as to signal him to shut up. The two just exchange a quick glance of disapproval in one another.

"Corey," she said. "I would love to be able to tell you more than you already know but I can't. You know as much as I do. There is still a third person out there. We are still trying to find the identity of John Doe number two at this point."

The waiter finally broke the conversation. "Ma'am what can I bring you to drink?"

"Water with lemon please," She said.

The waiter sat a menu in front of her and walked off. "You know guys; the only thing that is bothering me about this one is the fact that no one saw anything." She shook her head while looking over the menu.

14

Mark asked. "What happened to them? I haven't read the paper." He glanced over to Corey smugly.

"I don't know why I even look at this thing I will order the same thing I always do." She looked up at the two as the waiter brought the water with lemon and a straw.

"Are you guys ready to order?" He asked the three.

"He and I will split the NY Strip lunch special, rare with mashed potatoes and broccoli." Mark said while shutting his menu and handing it over.

The waiter turned to Lacy and said, "For you Miss?"

She replied, "The Cobb salad with no bacon." She pushed the menu over to the waiter and squeezed a lemon into her water. The waiter took his notes and turned to begin preparation of the order.

"What were we talking about?" She said to her friends.

"What happened to the two men? Mark said.

"Oh yeah... I was called to a crazy scene where two bodies of young males in their late twenties were lying in an alleyway between two apartment buildings. There is some evidence there was a third person present. We even found a third blood sample on the street in a trail leading away but no match in the system for it. One was shot, and the other stabbed. The third person had to have been shot too.

SERUM

There were four bullets missing from the gun, but only three recovered in the body.

I can only assume that the third person took the gun and knife. They were both found in a dumpster a block away. The same blood for the third person was on the grip of the gun and the hilt of the knife. I just wish there was something more I could do to figure this whole mess out. It drives me crazy to leave a case unsolved. It keeps me up at night." She drank a gulp of water to wet her throat.

"What can anybody do in this case, Lacy? You have done all you can do. It is now up to the police to find who did this." Mark reached out his hand on top of the table to touch hers and provide some sort of comfort.

"If I don't do my job, the police have nothing to go on. I hand the police the information. They go out and arrest the person for it. If I don't do my job well, the police can't do theirs." Lacy took her hand back leaving Marks on the table.

"What more can you do?" Mark asked. "I mean, you have done more than most-medical examiners do."

"I have been thinking about something guys. I need your professional opinion Mark." She paused and turned to stare Corey in the eyes. "Corey this conversation never happened. I need your word."

Corey nodded in agreement not knowing if he would keep the word. He was always looking for a story for either the paper or the science fiction magazine he published short stories in, under the pen name, Gerrard Lawson.

"I have been doing some research and I have an idea. I need you both to hear me out before you start to judge or ask questions. I already know what you are going to say Mark; I just need to know you can keep it a secret. Attorney-client privilege and all." She looked sincere.

"If you know what I am going to say then why are you telling us? You didn't fall in love with another dead beat, did you? You are not moving him in? Oh God..." Mark sighed as she interjected.

"No, this is strictly about work. And I know not entirely ethical." As she spoke the word, ethical Mark raised his left eyebrow giving a slight sign that she has peaked his interest. He nodded, and Corey leaned in to hear what this was all about. She said one more word. "Reanimation."

At the thought, Corey busted out laughing. "Reanimation, he said. Like in Frankenstein?" He tried to contain himself, but he couldn't. The thought made him laugh historically; so much so that people began to stare at them.

Mark said with a look of disapproval. "Control yourself." He turned to focus on Lacy, "And yes you

SERUM

are right it is very unethical. Even if you could do something like that it doesn't mean you should."

She frowned. "I am not talking about anything more than an experiment. If I were to put it into use, I would obviously consult the AMA and FDA."

"Oh my God, you are serious." Mark placed both hands face down on the table looking at her in awe. Corey began laughing again.

Lacy's red haired temper flared. "I see that we can't have a professional conversation here." With that Corey began to snicker again thinking of the preposterous idea.

The waiter arrived with a tray and tray stand to deliver the food. He placed the two plates on the table and asked if there was anything else he could get the three. "57 steak sauce for me and A1 for him." Mark said in reply. The waiter turned to retrieve the items.

"Lacy do you know how you sound right now?" Mark asked

She took the fork from her rolled up napkin and jammed it in the salad with anger. "Yes, Mark I know it sounds crazy, but I still think it's possible. Think of all the cases that could be solved."

"Ok, we are not going to talk about this anymore. I don't want to have to testify at your sanity hearing." Mark said.

"Fine..." She said angrily jamming her fork in the salad.

"Let's change the subject." Mark added. "I sat in on an interesting case yesterday waiting on my case to be called."

"Oh yeah, what was it about?" Lacy said as if she cared at this point.

"A psychologist killed her patient with a coffee carafe while she visited him in jail. It was so crazy she had no defense." Mark said while separating the steak into two portions and dividing the baked potato in half.

The waiter came back by and brought the steak sauce and a pitcher of water to refill the glasses.

"What kills me, guys, is the fact that I can solve them all." Lacy said as the waiter was walking off ignoring the story Mark was trying to tell.

"You can't solve them all. This is New York City with eight million people. How in the world do you expect to solve every case and identify every victim?" Corey said while putting his A1 on his portion of the steak and over the baked potato. "We are reporting on at least five murders a day in our paper. Granted there are few that go unsolved because of smart criminals."

"That is true." Lacy said while settling her temper. "There are some smart people out there and they do give themselves away eventually."

SERUM

Lacy heard her phone buzzing in her purse. She fished out her iPhone and noticed a text message on the screen. It was from detective Cox. "I guess you guys are right. Detective Cox has found the identity of the second victim. He still has no lead on the third person though."

"See Lacy let the system work..." Mark said.

"I will guys, but this is just one of many cases that end like this. I would say at least one percent." She said with a disappointing sound in her voice.

Mark and Corey exchanged a look of discontent in their friend. Mark said, "If I only won ninety-nine percent of my cases I would be ecstatic. I would be ranked the best lawyer in New York."

"Well guys I will let the system work on this one. How is your steak?" Lacy said while taking a big bite of her salad.

Months and months passed and there was no answer in the case of the stabbing and shooting. Lacy, working on another case with detective Cox asked if there was any new information in the stabbing shooting case. He only replied that the department head decided to close it as a cold case. This was a punch to her gut. This was only the second case under her watch that has gone cold.

Being in this job and being elected by the people of New York, Lacy felt a responsibility to her constituents. She felt that two years into her tenure she had failed the people of New York twice. At thirty years of age, Lacy felt a heavy weight.

CHAPTER 3

CHRISTOPHER MCDONALD

Regardless of the case, or body on the slab, Lacy takes every Sunday off for herself. Not for religious reasons but a ritual to relax. Most Sundays she found herself hanging out with her two best friends, Mark and Corey.

This particular Sunday Lacy showed up with a bottle of good wine and The Devil Wears Prada on DVD from her collection of chic flicks.

"Right on time," Mark said as he opened the door. I just started baking the fish. Salmon is good with you right?"

"You know its Sunday, and I can do anything I want on a Sunday." She said as she walked in the door. "Hey Corey, how are you."

Before Corey could answer, Mark jumped in. "He is going to disappear for a month or maybe two."

"What..." She said.

"Stop being so dramatic Mark." Corey sighed as he got up off the sofa to give Lacy a hug. "He is freaking out because I want to do an undercover assignment." Mark huffed as he grabbed the bottle of while from Lacy's arm and headed to the kitchen with it.

"What type of assignment?" Lacy said while taking a seat next to him on the sofa. As she sat down she left her sandals under the end table. "Is it dangerous? Is that why he is freaking?"

"Ok... There is this big Hollywood actor living here in New York. Everyone says he is a big heroin

SERUM

addict. My paper wants someone to get close to his crowd and get the story on him." Cory said while gesturing flamboyantly.

"That is a horrible idea Corey. Why would you even consider it?" Lacy said.

"The pay is four hundred thousand for the story. Is that enough of a reason for you? Then we can adopt a child." Corey replied

Mark appeared with two full glasses of wine for Lacy and himself. "He thinks we can't make it on the, small change, of a defense attorney in this city. He thinks this stunt will make me ready to adopt a child and move to the suburbs. What he fails to think about is anyone else."

"I have to agree with Mark on this one. How would you even go about it? Where would you stay and how would you get close to the actor?"

Mark sat at the opposite end of the living room staring at Corey while he proceeded to tell the whole hair-brained idea to Lacy. "The actor obviously lives on the nice part of town. He is known to dress down and walk to the park. On the way, he is said to stop off at an ATM and grab the cash. He usually wears a hoodie so no one will recognize him. He heads to the park gets the goods and leaves. All I have to do is catch the bulk of this activity on a hidden camera. I have to live and associate with the crew of dealers and become one myself."

Mark lashed out. "Lacy is it just me or is he flipping crazy?"

"Corey this is dangerous. What will you do if you get found out by the druggies?" Lacy asked while taking a big sip of wine. "Will you be able to call in?"

Corey said. "If you yahoos would ever let me finish I have something that might be interesting to you. The police will be involved in this to some degree."

"Corey, I am a lawyer, and I use terms like 'some degree' all the time. How will the police be involved? I call bullshit on the police involvement." Mark said

"Well, they are doing their undercover job while I am doing mine." Cory responded.

"Jesus H Christ..." Mark shouted. "What are you going to do if they bust you too? You have no immunity like a police officer does. You will be locked up with the rest of the scum."

"Well, it's a great thing I married a lawyer." He said while getting up off the sofa. "I will go make my own glass of wine and check on the fish and potatoes."

Lacy looked at Mark shaking her head. "You are not going to be able to stop him, you know that, right?"

SERUM

"When he gets his mind set on something he goes for its head first. He never thinks of other people. I don't know what to do." Mark said while taking another sip of wine.

"When is this assignment going to start?" Lacy asked.

"He is telling me this the day before his crappy paper gives him his new identity and place to live." Mark said as he slammed the wine glass on the end table nearly breaking the stem. "God only knows what mess he will be living in."

"Look," Corey said reentering the room. "I am an adult. I have a degree in journalism. Mark, you and I have been together for five years married for three. That does not give you any say in what jobs I take or how much money I can make. I will do this with or without the support of the two of you." He looked taking a long pause to observe them both. Mark just shook his head and sighed. "Dinner is ready by the way."

At the table Mark had one last thing to say on the subject before he would finally concede, maybe. "Honey you are a little effeminate. They will eat you alive."

Corey paused and placed his full fork on his plate. "There are both gay drug dealers and gay drug addicts. If there were not we would never get the

26

good X every time we decide to go clubbing together." Corey cocked his head. "Match point." Corey went on eating.

Lacy looked over at Mark and gave a shrug like she had given up half an hour ago. She looked to Corey to say her one last thing before ending the subject. "Corey, you must find a way to let us know you are safe. Write us a postcard and stick it in the mail, or something, every couple of days so that we know you are okay.

"I can do that." He said looking at Mark smugly, knowing he had won. "So... Lacy are you still working on your reanimation project?" He chuckled a little looking at his plate.

"Actually, Corey I have been doing some research in my spare time. I think I know about how I could pull it off. I want to try it." Both Corey and Mark paused and looked up from their plates to see if she was serious. She never took her eyes off her plate. "I think a virus and radiation are the key. Then to counteract it using potassium to kill the brain for the rest of the autopsy."

Corey's mouth flung open in horror seeing she was not joking. Some fried red potatoes flew from his lips and landed back on his plate. "Here I thought I would be the crazy one tonight."

Lacy looked up to see the reaction on their faces. "Come on guys. I am just reanimating the head. Not the body. I don't even know if it will work."

SERUM

Mark put his fork down. "Lacy do not do this. I can't take you going to jail too. My husband and best friend. No! I draw the line. One of you has to give this whole hair-brained thing up."

"Well Mark, I am not related to you in any way. You can't tell me what to do. I won't go to jail. Like I said I don't even know if this will work. I just have an Idea. Nothing more than an Idea on how I will make this happen." Lacy picked up her glass with a smug attitude as she spoke.

"I give up!" Mark yelled. "I can't win. You two are both nuts. I quit." Mark stood up from the table and walked out of the dining area.

Lacy fallowed him. "Mark calm down." He went to the living room and pored a scotch from the wet bar. "What is wrong with you Mark?"

"Lacy I have been your best friend for ten years; freshman year. I can watch you do something stupid like this. I can't watch Corey do something stupid. One of you has to not do this. I know that neither of you will listen, regardless of my plea." Mark sat in the overstuffed wingback and started drinking his scotch.

Corey walked in to the room as Lacy responded. "Mark, I will not do anything stupid. I will not get caught. Corey will be safe and everything will be fine. Stop worrying.

Corey said, "I will write every day if that helps any."

Mark finished off his glass of warm scotch and looked blankly at them. "What am I going to do with the two of you? You guys will be the death of me. Lacy I don't know how you will protect yourself? You can't even use anything like that in court."

"Mark if you will just calm down I will explain everything. You too Corey, pour him another drink and sit." Lacy said.

Corey poured the scotch for Mark and made one for Lacy and himself.

"What I plan to do is take a virus that is predominantly central to the brain. That way I will not be animating any other parts beyond the head. After I try it I will counteract the effects by injecting a lethal dose into the brain stem. Boom the stiff is out again." While Lacy spoke Mark sipped his glass of scotch. "See after the corpse is back out I can finish the autopsy. And release him or her for burial."

"I want to be nearby when you do this. Do you understand?" Mark said with a quiver.

Lacy and Corey exchange a look and a grin, knowing they have won. "Ok Mark anything you say." Lacy replied.

"Corey, I want you to write me a postcard daily and do not skip one or I will be hunting you down. You won't have to worry about the druggies in the park.

SERUM

You will have me to contend with." Mark said as he got up from the chair.

"Yes sir!" Corey said.

"Now if you both excuse me I need to sleep." Mark walked toward the bedroom.

"I need to go anyway." Lacy said. "I have so much to plan for." She stood from the sofa and slipped on her sandals. "I have to get to the lab so I can prep some things for testing."

After Corey and Lacy said their goodbyes Lacy left. Instead of going to the lab she decided to go looking for a virus. She stopped by the city's largest medical center

CHAPTER 4

SERUM

After leaving Mark and Corey's apartment, Lacy stopped by New York Presbyterian Hospital. This is the largest hospital in New York City. Most stiffs come from this hospital. Lacy keeps her lab coat and credentials in her trunk. She had decided that she would go on an undercover Mission.

Sunday night at nine o'clock is not usually a busy time in an emergency room. This was never the case for New York City's largest hospital. When Lacy walked to the reception desk she was greeted by an obese woman staring down at a celebrity tabloid.

Not looking up from the paper the woman said, "Honey you will have to take a number." She then pointed a finger with an extremely long nail at a red number dispenser.

Lacy shook her head and held out her badge. "It's Doctor Miller not Honey, Honey." The woman looked up with that little bit of 'oh shit' on her face.

"Who are you here for?" The receptionist asked.

"Whoever is in charge? Will you buzz me back please?" Lacy didn't wait on a response and just headed to the door.

Once on the other side of the door she saw nothing but chaos. A number of people were on beds in the hall several were sitting on the floor waiting to be seen. Most of the patients looked poor cr lower class. There were several doctors working on a man in trauma room one. Lacy looked around and tried to take it all in. She had never seen so many people. Instantly she knew that this was the place to find exactly what she needed.

Dr. Miller was greeted by a middle-aged man with prematurely greying hair. "I am Dr. Shaw; how can I help the City's chief medical examiner?" He extended his hand to shake hers.

"I am trying to find the source of a virus. I thought by coming tonight it would not be so busy. I see that I was dead wrong." Lacy said while noticing his hand smelled like sanitizer.

"Oh, you could never predict a slow night. In a city with this population, it would be imposable. What viruses are you tracking and why?" He said signaling her to follow him to the pit. This is where lacy had to think quickly. She had only half planned this whole hair brained visit while driving from Mark and Corey's place.

"Well I have seen a number of cases coming to the morgue who have suffered from meningitis. It looks like that's not the cause of death but I want to be sure. I wanted to see what you guys might be seeing down here." She said this while walking to the administration station known there as the pit.

SERUM

"I am not sure how I can help you if you don't have specific cases for me to pull." Dr. Shaw wrinkled his brow while picking up a chart.

"Well I am more interested in cases you have here tonight." She positioned herself in front of him to make him focus on her.

"Dr. Miller I don't think we have any cases here tonight of meningitis, but I will look for you." Dr. Shaw placed the chart back in the pit and walked to the nearest computer. He swiped his badge to access the list of patents.

After a few moments, he looked at her. I don't see any patients here tonight with viral meningitis. I do have someone in triage with a concussion. We will more than likely do a spinal tap on him. You can also wait on some labs to come back from this infant we are treating. We should be getting the results back on his labs soon."

"Do you mind if I just hang around to see?" She shrugged her shoulders.

"I don't mind but I need you to refrain from seeing the patients. You are not a physician at this hospital and not authorized to assist." As he began the speech she held up her hands signaling she understood.

"I will just hang around the pit here and be patient." She grabbed the phone from the pocket and started fidgeting with it. She was trying to show she have something to do while she waited.

"I will be back when I get some results on the baby. In the meantime, have a seat and enjoy the show." Dr. Shaw chuckled as he walked off grabbing a chart as he left.

A show is exactly what Lacy got. She had so many people whirling around her. Nurses and paramedics rushing here and there. She picked up on things they were saying while running back and forth. She recognized the lingo but not the pace. She could probably do four autopsies in one day. If pushed she could do five. These people were working on ten people at once.

She overheard one of the nurses talking about the infant's labs. "The baby in room three is about to get discharged."

Lacy spoke up. "Oh... What did the poor thing have?"

The nurse looked up recognizing she was looking at a doctor said, "Meningitis."

Lacy perked up and said, "Poor dear."

The two nurses scattered and Lacy headed to room three. Room three was just across from the pit where she was standing. As she approached she heard the uncomfortable sound of a baby crying. She knocked on the door twice and went in. She found two very concerned parents and an infant in a car seat on the table.

SERUM

"Who are you? Do you have answers? Why won't she stop crying?" The apparent father said.

"I'm Dr. Miller," Without thinking Lacy gave her title, "I'm the city's Chief Medical Examiner."

The mother jumped from her seat lunging for Dr. Miller. "My baby is not dying!" She screamed as she lunged onto Lacy. This made Lacy jump and recant her statement.

"Noooo…. Your child is fine and completely curable. I just want a sample of her spinal fluid." Lacy said while patting the sobbing mother on the back.

"What!" The father yelled. "You want what? Spinal fluid?"

"Yes, please don't be alarmed. It is for some research I am doing regarding deaths in the city these last couple months." Lacy let the mother go as she spoke.

Both parents looked at lacy and said in unison. "Don't be alarmed!"

Dr. Shaw had been standing at a partially cracked door listing to the latter half of the conversation. As he walked in he said, "Dr. Miller, you beat me here. I was just going to tell the parents of this beautiful child that I am prescribing an antibiotic and sending her home."

Dr. Miller looked puzzled. "The meningitis is bacterial?"

"Yes Dr. Miller, bacterial." Dr. Shaw replied.

"Well in that case I am so sorry to bother you." Dr. Miller said. "I was looking for viral meningitis. Sorry for the trouble."

Dr. Shaw nodded to the door and began to comfort the parents and inform them that the full recovery would be around ten days. Lacy left the room feeling at a loss thinking she had really screwed this one up.

After Lacy returned to the pit she was met by Dr. Shaw a few minutes later. "What the hell were you doing going in there like that?"

"I was only trying to get a sample for my study and epidemical research." Dr. Miller looked truly sorry witch put Dr. Shaw at ease. "You know what... If you get a case of viral meningitis please call me." She pulled out her card and handed it to him.

"I would thank you for stopping by." He said in reply.

It had been a couple years sense she had dealt with live people and their families. She walked out of the ER and past the receptionist with an attitude. She pondered the subject in her mind. What she had done wrong

.

2

SERUM

A couple of days passed and Lacy received the call she had hoped for from Dr. Shaw. "Dr. Miller, I have a patient here with viral meningitis caused from herpes simplex. She will be admitted for treatment. If you would like to come by and chat with her you are more than welcome."

When Lacy arrived at the hospital she went through something similar with a new receptionist. Lacy thought that they must have had the same trainer. For a Wednesday at noon you could almost hear a pin drop in the ER.

"Is she still here or did you move her to a room?" Lacy asked as she approached Dr. Smith.

"Well hello to you, too, Dr. Miller." Dr. Shaw said with a sarcastic tone. "She is still here in the ER. She comes in complaining of headaches and nausea. We did a CT and noticed the swelling. We did a spinal tap to confirm. It came back viral."

"Great let's go see her." Lacy said with her perky voice.

Dr. Shaw threw up his hand. "I need to give you more detail about..."

Lacy cut him off. "I just need some of her spinal fluid. The rest is irrelevant."

Dr. Shaw gestured with a 'follow me' gesture. He led her to the room of the patient. When they walked in the room Dr. Miller was introduced. "Jenna this is Dr. Miller. She is conducting some research on the virus that is infecting you."

Dr. Miller looked the woman up and down. She was wearing a hospital gown provided by the hospital. She had short dingy hair Missing teeth and a smoker's voice. "Well hey there Dr. Miller. You goanna help me nab the John who gave me the herps?"

"I can't match the virus exactly. The man who gave you this was named John?" Dr. Miller looked at Dr. Shaw with a shrug. Learning from her past mistakes. She didn't want to scare this one off.

"No Dr. Miller... John is what we working girls like to call a client." Jenna adjusted the bed so that she was almost sitting up.

"Oh, you are a prostitute?" As the words come out of her mouth you could hear the slap of Dr. Shaw's hand against his forehead.

Jenna blinked a couple time before she responded. "Man, you got some brass. Yes, I'm a prostitute. I also smoke crack so I guess you can call me a crack whore."

"I meant no offense. I haven't been dealing with many..." She paused to choose her words. She didn't want to say dead people and scare her off. "...Working women."

"It's okay," Jenna replied. "I come to terms with it years ago. This is the life I fell into when I ran away from home all those years ago. At first, I told

SERUM

myself I would do it long enough to put back some cash. I never left it. I was hooked on the dope and the sex."

This made Lacy feel some form of sadness for Jenna. She had never had to make the choices that she had made. She never thought about what might drive a person to end up in a situation like this. "I wish there was something I could do to make your life better," Lacy said.

"Honey at this point there is nothing you can do. I also have HIV. I'm done. If this doesn't kill me the next thing will." Jenna began to cough.

Dr. Miller looked at Dr. Shaw it was a look that told him she now knew what he was trying to tell her in the hall. She turned her focus back on Jenna. "Jenna there is something I need from you for my research. I need to get a sample of your cerebral spinal fluid."

Jenna said "Huhhh?" She gave a puzzled look to Dr. Shaw standing in the doorway.

Dr. Shaw answered, "You know the test we did where we put the needle in your back to get some liquid."

Jenna remembered this and remembered well. "Absolutely not! NO no no no." She crossed her arms and shook her head as she spoke. "That was the most painful test I have ever had done. I will not do that one again. I would rather die."

"I can numb you up before I do it." Lacy said.

"Yeah that's what the other bitch said. I think she numbed herself up and still stuck me. No Miss you will not stick me in the back with another needle. I could be paralyzed in addition to everything else wrong with me." Jenna emphatically said. She started coughing uncontrollably.

"If you could just let me try." Dr. Miller said. Jenna waived her hand in the air while she was hacking as if to dismiss Dr. Miller. Dr. Shaw approached the bedside handing Jenna her cup of water.

"Dr. Miller I will see you in the hall." He motioned his head for her to exit while he tended to the spastic patient. Lacy did as instructed and walked to the hall. She could still hear the conversation happening in the room. "Jenna, I will talk with her. If you change your mind about the lumbar puncture it could help save someone's life. And the site we get the sample from does not have your spinal cord in it, but I will leave and let you rest."

As she began to calm down the coughing she said. "It's not goanna happen Doc. You can tell that hoity-toity bitch no for me."

On that note Dr. Shaw turned to walk out of the room. He shut the door as he left to insure she could not hear the conversation between him and Dr. Miller. "I will give you a call if she changes her mind. I can't guarantee that she will, but we can hope."

SERUM

Dr. Shaw turned to walk away. "Dr. Shaw, I'm a hugger" Lacy said as she stretched her arms out wide. Dr. Shaw looked perplexed at this grown professional woman wanting to give him a goodbye hug. Even though he found this extremely odd he indulged her giving a halfhearted hug and a pat on the back.

"Like I said I will call you if she changes her mind." Dr. Smith turned and started walking down the hall.

"Thanks again Dr. Smith." Lacy shouted as she placed his ID badge in her front lab coat pocket.

Lacy headed to the nearest door that might lead to the inner most part of the hospital. She began to walk around aimlessly. This hospital was not arranged like the one she had interned in. This was an older part of the hospital that was being refurbished. The hall she found herself in smelled of fresh paint. She began to look for the lab. Passing sign after sign pointing one direction or another she felt like she was going in circles.

She thought she should have planned the heist of the ID card better. It was a stupid spur of the moment thing but she needed to get the active virus one way or the other. She felt that any moment Dr. Shaw would realize his badge was gone and send the hounds after her. She felt like she was getting close as she passed a waiting room Marked x-ray.

CHRISTOPHER MCDONALD

She finally made it to the lab waiting room. She passed by the entrance slowly so she could case the joint. There was only one person sitting at the check-in desk and only one elderly man sitting in the waiting room. Lacy passed by noticing two doors about ten yards from the waiting room on the same side of the hall. Two women in blue scrubs came out of the doors caring clipboards. She decided this was her way in. She comes to the door just after it closed and placed her stolen badge on the card reader. The reader beeped and a green light lit up. She was in.

The environment was the same as any other research lab. Several testing tables with microscopes and bulky equipment on either side. She went to the large case with glass doors. Inside the refrigerated case were vials upon vials of blood samples. She was able to narrow down the spinal fluid samples quickly she began to sift through the thirty or forty samples. After pulling a few out she noticed all they had were patient numbers on them with no names. The only name was the physician that ordered the test. She didn't now how to sift through the database to find the one she needed so she improvised. In the interest of time she pulled every vial with Dr. Shaw's name on it and put it in her pocket. She ended up with at least seven vials out of the selection.

She closed the door as quietly as possible and began to walk to the door. "Can I help you with

SERUM

something?" a woman's voice said from the other end of the lab.

Lacy looked up startled not knowing how much the woman had seen of her heist. "Oh no dear. I just come to check on a sample I collected. I wanted to make sure there was enough to run one more test. You don't want to make the patient more uncomfortable than we have to."

Lacy noticed the woman was not a lab tech but a receptionist and this seemed to satisfy her. "Okay doctor." The woman said and went in to the next room.

This was a close one for Lacy and she knew the longer she stayed in the hospital the higher the chance was she would be discovered. She darted for the door when the woman turned to leave and pressed the exit button. In the hall, she looked to the celling. Following the exit signs, she made it to the lobby for outpatient surgery. Once out the two sliding glass doors she dumped the stolen ID in the nearest trash can.

It was on the way to her lab when she realized the severity of what she had done. If she were caught she would lose her license, be fired, and possibly jailed. The thought made her stomach ache. She told herself it was for the good of New York City.

CHAPTER 5

SERUM

Corey started his Monday morning bright an early loading up a cab at 8am with some suitcases and his undercover gear. It consists of a camera system that was built in to a button. Mark and Corey said their goodbyes outside the apartment building.

Climbing in to the back seat of the cab he said, "I have already predated and stamped thirty postcards to drop in the mail every day. You should get your first here in a couple of days. I love you."

Mark looking as if has tearing up said, "I love you too. You better be safe you little bastard."

With that Corey told the address to the driver and he left Mark on the curb outside their home. The cab ride was relatively uneventful. Cory checked his briefcase to make sure he didn't accidentally throw his cell phone in there out of habit. He remembered he had strict orders to cut all ties with family and friends. He did not want to do anything that might tip off one of the druggies that he was undercover.

When the cab stopped outside the twenty something unit building Corey got a sick feeling in his stomach. The building was in disrepair and several windows had portable air conditioners rigged up to them. "That will be fifteen-fiddy" The cab driver said interrupting his thoughts.

"Here is a twenty keep the change." Corey said while pulling out a twenty from envelope with three thousand dollars in it. Corey grabbed up his briefcase and his pull behind luggage and stepped to the curb. Again, he stared long and hard at the building he was about to call home for a month maybe two. Okay buddy you can do this. Just keep telling yourself four hundred thousand dollars.' He grabbed up his bags and went inside.

He noticed walking in to lobby that there was a smell that permeated the place. It was something like the smell you smell in an old-folks home. He looked around before walking in to the office. The Lobby was quiet. Mail boxes to one side. A large wooden staircase and an office. It looked that behind the office was an apartment but he couldn't tell.

He walked into the office to find a man watching an I love Lucy rerun on the old tube TV set next to the front desk. "Hi," Corey said to the man watching the TV. "I understand you have a furnished efficiency for rent."

The man looked up at Corey and said. "Buddy think you are in the wrong part of town." He looked Corey up and down trying to figure out if he was serious.

"No, I think I am in the right part of town. I just come from Iowa and just getting started in the city. I need a place to stay." Corey folded his arms and

SERUM

placed them on the counter indicating that he was not leaving until he got a place.

"Alrighty then," the man said reaching under the counter for a clipboard with some paperwork. "Fill this out. I'm the owner of the building. You can call me Mr. Bill." He stuck his hand out to shake Corey's hand but to also see if he had needle Marks on his arm. Bill had been dealing rooms to junkies for some time. He knew by the Marks on the arm, if any, whether they would be paying on time.

"I'm Corey..." He thought long and hard before answering. He had chosen another last name for the assignment and he wanted to make sure he got it right from the get go. "Corey Avery. It's a pleasure to meet you Mr. Bill."

"This is an easy place to live as long as you don't start bringing in trouble to the building. Keep your drama out there." He said wile pointing to the front door.

"I understand." Corey said while filling out his paperwork.

"The rent on the rooms here are the same for everyone. Three hundred a week paid every Friday before five PM. Starting Saturday at noon I start taking your stuff to the street and the for-rent sign goes back up. Other than that, do you have any questions before we look at the unit?" Mr. Bill reached in his pocket for a large key ring so that he would be able to show the unit.

"No that sounds reasonable enough to me. I will make sure I pay on time." Corey signed the bottom of the not so legal rental agreement and handed over his newly printed fake New York ID.

"Wow I thought you said you come from Iowa." Mr. Bill looked at him then back at the ID.

I have been in New York for a couple of weeks living out of cheap motels. I got it as soon as I came to the city." Corey felt nervous he was about to be found out on his first day as Corey Avery.

Mr. Bill looked suspiciously at him. "You got a job?" Mr. Bill put his licensee in the all-in-one printer copier.

Over the hum of the scanner working Corey replied, "yes sir. I just started waiting tables at Guston's." Again, something told him Mr. Bill smelled the bull shit from a mile back.

Maybe it was because he was a clean looking guy. Mr. Bill seemed willing to take the leap. "Let's go up and make sure this is what you want."

"Sounds great." Corey replied as he put the last signature on the forms.

Mr. Bill jingled the keys in his hands and motioned for them to step out of the office. "Let me just lock up. You can leave your bags in here if you would like. They should be safe." Mr. Bill and Corey stepped out of the small office.

SERUM

Bill said while locking the office. "The only unit I have available is on the fifth floor. You look like a spring chicken though you should be fine."

"I'm older than I look, but I guess it will have to do." Corey said following Mr. Bill to the stairs. The old wooden stairs had to have been a hundred years old. The wood creaked as they walked up all five floors. At the top Mr. Bill paused to catch his breath. For a man of his size he did well considering.

At the top, there were four doors. Two on each side of the landing. Pointing at one Bill said, "501 front facing view." He went over and started counting through the keys. As he swung open the door. "It's not much but for three-hundred it's a place to call home."

They both stepped in. To Corey's amazement the apartment was all just one room. Not at all what he expected. Even the sink and toilet were out in the open. There was a stove and small icebox. A twin sized bed pressed up against the opposite wall from the appliances. Corey noticed while looking at the bed he would have to go shopping. There were no sheets and he didn't bring any. He only had clothes and his toiletries.

Bill broke the silence. "It's not much, like I said. Again, it is only three Benjamins a week. I inherited the building from my grandmother six years ago and never gone up on rent once. I have, on the other hand, had trouble with some crack-heads not paying. So, what do you say?"

Corey stared at the space long and hard asking himself if he should back out of this whole thing. Telling himself, 'four hundred thousand.' "Okay Mr. Bill I will take it," he said with a little hesitation in his voice."

"Well good. Let's head back down and I will get you a key." Bill headed out the door and Corey reluctantly followed.

As they descended the stairs Corey began to second guess things. Thinking to himself 'What am I doing? How is a gay man going to survive in this room for a month? How in the world will I ever get in to the business?'

As they reached the bottom of the stairs Mr. Bill unlocked the door and they both went in. "So, you want the box, right?"

"Yes, I will take the box and all of its contents." Corey propped himself on the front counter.

"Ok then, I have the paperwork and all I need is the three hundred bucks." Mr. Bill slapped his hand on the counter startling Corey.

"Yeah, let me see. My briefcase?" Corey fumbled around trying to remember what he had done with the cash. He found his briefcase and the envelope. Realizing what sort of area, he was in he knew he had to be more careful going forward with

SERUM

this much cash. He pulled out three one-hundred dollar bills and laid them on the counter next to Mr. Bill's hands.

Bill wrinkled his brow and looked at the money. "Wow did you just print these up or something?" He held each bill to the light looking for the strip and the hologram. "They look legit. Sorry but I am used to people paying in ones and fives."

Corey looked at him strange and pushed the envelope of cash as deep as he could in his briefcase. "So... I guess all I need is the key"

Bill looked up like he himself had forgotten. "Give me a sec and I will fetch you one." Bill turned and walked through the doorway behind the counter. There was some clanking around then a grinding noise. Corey realized that he had to make a key from his master.

Bill surfaced after a couple of minutes with the freshly made keys. He blew on the keys to insure no shavings were left. "Here ya go buddy." He slapped two keys on the counter, one larger than the other. "The small one is your box key. You are box twenty-five."

Corey picked up the keys and stuffed them in his front pocket. "Is that everything? I need to go out and get some sheets and things."

"Nope... I hope you enjoy your time here." Mr. Bill paused like there more he wanted to let Corey know about the building. Instead of warning him Bill bit his tongue. He didn't want to scare the only perspective clean person out of his building.

After making his way back to the fifth floor he felt out of breath. 'This will be the best way for me to get my exercise in.' Corey told himself while he placed the newly minted key in the door of the dump he would call home for at least four weeks.

Once inside he latched the deadbolt and chain lock. Looking around he felt ill. This was his first time alone. He has always lived with someone. Corey knew that he had jumped head first in the deep end all over some cash. 'Four hundred thousand'

Looking around the room, he needed to find an inconspicuous place to hide his cash. That would blow his cover quicker than anything if someone were to look in the freezer and find thousands stashed there. He thought about the mattress and knew it was a cliché from the beginning. He looked over at the toilet. "What if I cot a baggie and put it in the tank?" He said out loud to himself.

He walked over and took the lid off the back of the toilet and peered in. Knowing instantly that this was not going to be his hiding place. The inside of the tank had black looking algae and barnacle looking growths. "No sir. Corey, you will not be putting your hands in that tank."

SERUM

Looking around the one room he knew he would have to be a little more creative. The radiator would get too hot. The stove is just dumb. When he looked at it he knew. The one drawer and one cabinet door between the stove and sink. He pulled the empty drawer all the way out and flipped it over. He decided he would tape the envelope to the back of the drawer. Someone would really have to be in the mood for a spatula to find it there. Now it's just a matter of heading to the local Walgreens to get some tape with his spatula.

Having a game plan now Corey decided it was time to get some supplies for his new home. All the supplies he got would have to be burner supplies. He would need to be able to ditch them quickly. Before walking down stairs he placed the cash in two stacks in each of his front pockets to try not draw attention to a pocket bulge. He left the apartment locking up to protect his undercover gear and his clothes.

2

After arriving at the local Walgreens that afternoon he grabbed a buggy. He was lucky that Walgreens carried a little of everything you might need. He started off, like most gay men, looking for personal hygiene products. Picking up the essential razor, toothbrush, toothpaste soap and shampoo. He decided he would take the assignment seriously and act like someone just moving to the city.

Moving from aisle to aisle he picked off staples for his new apartment. Grabbing a shower curtain, toilet paper, and duct tape to hold his money envelope. He skipped the food section figuring he would mostly be eating outside the apartment. He on the other hand grabbed some cleaning supplies and some Febreze for the carpet and the mattress.

Taking his overflowing buggy to the counter the clerk asked, "Did you find everything you needed?"

Corey answered, "Actually no. I need a pre-paid cell phone."

"Oh, we have those here behind the counter." The clerk pointed at three different phones on a shelf next to the Marlboro cartons. "The Verizon flip phone is fifty bucks and comes with fifty dollars in air time to use so it's like getting it for free."

"I will take that one then," Corey said while placing handful of items at a time on the counter to be scanned.

"You must have just moved here. You needed everything." The clerk observed while placing the items in a bag.

SERUM

"Yep..." Corey placed bags back in the buggy and shoveled more stuff to the counter top. "Iowa. I'm here on hoping to find work. Got here last night in fact."

"Well if you are looking for work all you have to do is walk the streets around here. You are bound to see a help wanted sign in the window of a coffee shop or a restaurant." The clerk finished bagging the last of the purchases. He grabbed the Verizon phone from the counter behind him rang it in and tossed it in the bag. "Anything else, sir?"

"No that should do it. I have enough to haul up to the fifth floor as it is." Thinking now of having to make several trips with nine bags of crap made him sick to his stomach.

"That will be two-hundred and fifteen dollars and fifty-two cents." As the clerk said the total Corey's eyes bulged in amazement that he had spent so much at Walgreens. He now had to get this stuff home and go out again for linens.

Corey pulled from his pocket a wad of bills. Trying not to be flashy with it he counted three one-hundred dollar bills and handed them over to the clerk. He was embarrassed looking back to see a long line forming behind him. He would have asked the clerk for help calling a cab but decided not to give the line forming.

Corey loaded his buggy to the brim and walked to the automatic doors. With a whooshing noise, they opened to busy street with lunchtime traffic just getting started. With the buggy next to him he waived his hand to hail a taxi. No driver wanted to stop. Car after car passed him by while he tried to hail a cab. Finally, someone did pull up to the curb next to the Walgreens.

A Middle Eastern man jumped out of the bright yellow taxi and went around to open the trunk. "You need help sir?" He asked with a thick Middle Eastern accent and while holding the trunk of the Crown Vic.

"Yes, I do thank you so much." Corey wheeled the cart over to the back of the cab. The driver and Corey began loading the trunk with his purchases when the noise of a thunderclap came.

"I think I made it to you just in time sir. The rain is inevitable." The driver slammed the trunk lid of the Crown Vic and went to the driver's door. 'I will wait for you to take buggy in." and he jumped in the cab trying to beat the rain.

Corey pushed the buggy into the whooshing doors as the rain began to fall. He always loved the rain but this was a bit much. The rain came down so hard that by the time he had reached the cab he was drenched.

"I'm glad we got your stuff loaded before the free shower came." The diver chuckled as Corey

SERUM

jumped in the cab. To say the least Corey was not amused by the statement but glad he stopped.

After returning to his new apartment building the rain had subsided to a slight drizzle. Corey gave twenty-five bucks to the driver and went around to the trunk. The driver met him with an umbrella. 'Where was this earlier?' Corey thought to himself.

The driver helped set his bags on the street curb and thanked him for the tip. Now Corey had the daunting task of lugging the nine bags plus a large pack of toilet paper up the five flights of stairs. Corey managed to fit all nine bags on his two arms. He thought 'This is heavy as fuck,' as he kicked the package of toilet paper to the building entrance.

This building did not have a door man to help. Corey had to manage on his own. Huffing and a puffing the whole way through the door, he made it. 'How the hell am I going to last a whole month if I can't even manage this on my own?' He thought.

Leaving the package of toilet paper by the door he decided to sprint up the stairs. It was on floor three he was sadly out of breath. The next two floor he took in stride trying (without success) to catch his breath.

He reached the top floor and practically collapsed in front of his apartment door wheezing from exhaustion. 'How the hell am I going to last a month, assuming I can get the job done by then?'

After catching his breath, he opened the door shoving his purchases inside. He then descended the stairs to retrieve his last parcel next to the buildings entrance. 'Given my luck someone will have swiped it by the time I get there.' Even though it was plausible that someone could have stolen his ass wiping paper he found it just where he left it.

He paused at the floor of the stairs with the toilet paper under his arm thinking. 'Why could I not find a building with an elevator and a door man? Oh yeah that's right I am supposed to be hanging out with the drug crowd.' He started back up the stairs thinking out loud this time. "You stupid fuck face. What were you thinking?"

Once back in the apartment Corey opened the Verizon pre-paid cell phone box. 'Burner phone, burner apartment, burner identity, what's next? Oh yeah, a burner job in the drug trade. I still don't know how I am going to do that.'

Corey left the apartment after activating his new LG flip phone. He was still in amazement that people still used these things. He thought of who he might call now that he has a line of communication as he descended the five floors of his building. He realized the only number he could remember was the seven digits of his mother's   home in Maine. The town was so small growing up he never had to use an

SERUM

area code. 'It's funny,' he thought. 'My iPhone remembers all my numbers so I don't have too.'

Once out the door to his new building he looked out at the freshly drenched street. The rain was gone but the sky had yet to clear. There was steam rising from the pavement as the heat from the cars worked on evaporating the residual rain.

This time Corey had no problem hailing a cab. He raised a hand and one comes right for him. He instructed the driver to take him to the nearest department store. He may be in a shit hole of an apartment for a month, but he would not sleep on bad sheets.

He arrived at Macy's department store and went straight for the home goods section. He searched for a good while until he found on a clearance rack a bed in a bag set by Ralph Lauren. 'Six hundred thread count should do.' The set was pale blue and for a twin bed. He went and grabbed a memory foam pillow and a couple of Ralph Lauren white towels and washcloths. The total for his purchase, even with the bedding set on clearance, was nearly two hundred dollars.

3

Once back at the apartment Corey began to unpack everything. He decided he would take a shower go and eat a sensible meal. Then head over to the park for employment opportunities. Still not sure how he needs to get into the business he brings out his printouts on Google.

If the FBI really wanted to find the crooks they should be tracking the Google search request of everyone. He had a printout that led him to a story of heroin from the New York Times (A much more credible paper than his). The article gave statistics on the drug trafficking in the city. From the article, he notices that Hispanics account for sixty percent of the distribution.

'So, what am I going to do? Walk up to the first Hispanic in the park and ask how to get some smack? (Another Google search pulled up some street names)' He thought while hanging his plane white shower curtain. 'This is going to be harder than I thought.'

After the shower, he put on a polo shirt and some cargo shorts. Corey fixes the button camera to his polo and slides on some Old Navy flip-flops. He looked like a twenty-one-year-old kid not the thirty something trying to work undercover. He takes one

SERUM

thousand dollars from his stash and tapes the rest to the back of the kitchen drawer as planned.

Once outside the building with nothing but a thousand in cash and burner phone he decided to walk and take in the people of the neighborhood while looking for a place to eat. Walking down the street he notices his building is not the only slum unit building on the street. This just happened to be the only one advertising on Craig's List.

There were kids of every background playing in the alleyways between the buildings. Most of them enjoying the post-rain heat. Passing by another building he notices two African women sitting on the steps outside their building. He knew they must be from Africa because it sounded like Swahili they were speaking. One woman sat in front of the other on the steps braiding her hair. As Corey passed by, they stopped talking, and stopped braiding, to stare at him. He never felt so out of place in his life.

He comes to a major intersection of streets. He noticed to his right there were businesses lit up in all of their neon. Package stores, paycheck cashing, title pawn, they were all lit up. He was more interested in the red awning with the black Chinese lettering on it a block away. His stomach began to growl at the possibility that it was a Chinese restaurant.

As he approached he found that he was right. It was an authentic Chinese restaurant. The people who greeted him at the door were Chinese (Or so he assumed). The dining room was furnished in an overdone oriental style. Because of the time of day, he was only one of a few guests in the entire dining area.

He was seated at a table off to himself and ordered an ice tea. The Waitress placed a menu on the table and said, "Will be back."

Looking over the menu Corey knew what he wanted. He was a creature of habit and connoisseur of Mongolian Beef. He liked to try it at every Chinese restaurant he encountered. Looking around he noticed an oriental looking family sitting at a round table sharing a large plate of crab legs. Behind them was a fish tank with lobster and Dungeness crab crawling around.

The waitress returned with his tea and asked, "You order now." He thought she was asking anyway. He noticed her teeth were blackened in the front and made him slightly uneasy about eating here.

"I will take the Mongolian Beef with white rice. Also, I would like a cup of egg drop soup." Corey placed his straw in the drink while ordering.

"Oh, ok ok... Will be back." She said as she headed to the two stainless steel doors at the back of the dining room.

SERUM

Corey pondered on their national origin. Were they really Chinese or were they from some other Asian country? Coming to America to escape oppression from their government and fell into the role of Chinese restaurant owners.

Corey realized that if he come out of this empty handed he can at least us some of this material from his experiences for the mystery rag. 'The Asian Mafia' he thought, chuckling to himself. The thought that his waitress with the bad teeth could be a Mafioso made him chuckle harder. The laughing caught the attention of the family dining on crab in the corner. They all stopped what they were doing to turn and stare at him. He immediately stopped the giggle fit thinking, 'I guess the idea wasn't too farfetched by the looks of it.'

The woman soon returned with the soup in a blue and white printed cup with matching saucer. After thanking her he poured some pepper over the soup and brought some to his lip to check the temperature. At first sip his tongue was set ablaze. His sinus cavity began to burn. This time the coughing that ensued didn't bother the table of crab crackers. The coughing did, on the other hand, grab the attention of the waitress.

After coming to the table she said, "Oh sir, this is white pepper. Berry spicy." She said this with a smug look and smirk on her face.

After drinking big gulps of his tea, he looked at her with tears in his eyes. "I think I just figured it out the hard way. I will be okay, thank you."

The waitress walked away while he tried his best to scoop some of the pepper off the top that was still floating. 'I think they are in the Chinese military with that stuff.' He thought to himself while gathering his composure.

The Mongolian beef arrived. He decided not to put any of the condiments on his table on his meal. By the time he finished and paid he was wondering how much crab that one family could hold. They were there when he come in and are still cracking and eating as he was ready to pay and leave. He left a ten and five on the table for the waitress while he went to the restroom before leaving.

The restrooms were to the left of the double stainless-steel kitchen doors. As he passed by, he smelled something almost sweet and pungent at the same time. He also smelled something that resembled plastic burning. The smells were strange coming from the kitchen. He couldn't quite make them out.

4

SERUM

Leaving the Chinese Mafia behind, Corey decided to find one of these neighborhood parks he read about online. The most logical thing in his mind was to start small in the neighborhood or close to it. He needed to find a place where he could get in good. He knew after he got in with the local dealers he could move up or down and find the real skid row. He just hoped he could get all of this done before the end of the month. He was not feeling like staying undercover for more than that.

He figured he would enter the scene and no one would suspect anything when he just disappeared. 'Just another junkie.' He imagined they will say. 'Probably in jail or something.' No one would Miss him.

After walking a couple blocks he came across an alley. It was dark and tight between two tall buildings. He heard someone talking in the distance. He couldn't see them or make out what was being said but he knew it was human communication. He stood there at the end of the alley and contemplated.

It reminded him of the case Lacy was working on, the one where no one knew the killer. The person with the gun. Corey stood at the end of the alley looking in while other just walked past on their normal Monday routine. He thought of what might happen if he were to just walk down there. Just see what all the talking was about. Then the case Lacy was working on surfaced. Would he be yet another faceless person on the coroner's slab? Or would he be smart and keep walking.

Corey stood there for at least ten minutes. He mustered up the courage thinking, 'The sooner I get this over with the sooner I can go home to Mark and adopt a baby.' He slowly walked into the darkness easing closer to the conversation. He heard the two men speaking and speaking fast. He quickly realized they were in the middle of a domestic argument. In addition, they were speaking Spanish. He took Spanish in college but could only pick up on every other word.

Corey realizing that he would get nowhere here turned and headed to the light of the street once again. He continued down the street passing stores with neon signs like, Check Cashing Here!, We Buy Gold!, Title Pawn. By the looks of things, he was in the right neighborhood. He decided to look in on a Check cashing place next to a package store.

Inside the Check cashing place were two men in line. One was someone Corey picked up on that he needed to follow for some time. He was in shabby clothes and was shifting his weight back and forth while the man in the suit cashed his payroll check. Corey decided he would walk in and get in line behind the two men.

"Come on man." The homeless looking man said shifting his weight. Corey noticed he had a check

SERUM

with the Statue of Liberty on it. It was a check from the U.S. Government. 'Most likely a disability payment.' Corey thought. He was right. The man plopped the check on the counter and slid it under the two-inch-thick security glass.

Corey read the rates of the check cashing on the sign above the security glass. A government check was listed at five percent. If you put it on a prepaid card you got it for the great rate of three percent. Something told Corey he would be taking it in cash and probably be broke by tomorrow or the next day.

Corey watched as the transaction come to a close and the casher placed the cash under the slot in the window. The man was in such a hurry he didn't even pick up his coins, just the cash. The attendant said. "Next please." By this time there was another person behind him.

Corey replied trying to get out as to follow the man. "Oh... I'm sorry I forgot my ID."

The casher said, "That's not a problem here sir."

Corey still turned and ignored the attendant thinking, 'How does a place stay in business without verifying the identification of the person cashing the check.' The reality was they did not care if the check was given legitimately or not they were just there to make their five percent and move on with the day.

CHRISTOPHER MCDONALD

Corey popped out of the tiny store front looking for his check cashing homeless man. He looked left then right and didn't immediately see him. The homeless man had jutted across the street and was heading downtown. After picking him up again Corey went into a power walk to make up the time. The man was definitely on a Mission with his couple hundred in his pocket.

Corey thought he would feel real stupid if he was wasting all of this energy and the man was not after drugs. What if the man were rushing to pay an electric bill before the lights were cut off? Corey then realized his profile of the man and initial assessment was that he was homeless. He didn't think people had light bills under the overpass or bridge.

When Corey was a couple yards behird the man he slowed his pace again realizing how cut of shape he was. He continued to tail the man until he veered into a public park. Corey thought, 'Now we are getting somewhere.' Parks are where he read most of this happens.

The man walked down the center path and stopped at a large oak tree in the center of the park. Corey sat on a bench about a hundred yards away keeping all eyes on his homeless guy. This park was full of trees and dog walking trails. He sat watching women pushing baby strollers talking on their cell phones.

SERUM

Hours passed and the man just paced outside the restroom. No one stopped to talk to him and no one engaged him in conversation. He just walked in circles. Corey thought to himself, 'I have followed a nut job thinking he was going to buy drugs. I went down a dark alley thinking someone was dealing drugs. This job is going to take more time than I thought.'

As dusk began to fall Corey began to contemplate giving up on home and heading back to the apartment to regroup and re plan a better strategy for tomorrow. As the street lights in the park lit up Latino looking man walked from behind the restroom building. He obviously didn't use the typical paths in and out of the park. Corey watched in amazement as what he thought of as a drug deal was happening. He struggled to cut on the camera mounted on his shirt.

The Latino man took a blue bag out of his pocket. The bag was small. So, small in fact Corey thought there could not possible be anything in it at all. Corey needed to move closer without being seen by the two. He walked through the dog walk that was not lit. He got within three hundred feet of the two.

Corey overheard the conversation. "It was only twenty a gram last month." The homeless man said.

The Latino responded, "Homie it changes depending on demand. You know that. It's twenty-five this week." The Latino dangled the little blue bag that obviously had a powdery substance in it.

This whole scenario was everything Corey had expected. A Hispanic selling smack to a junkie. 'Now how do I get in on it?' He thought. 'I can't just walk up and say Hi Mr. drug dealer.'

The junkie left the Latino man behind. Corey waited another minute and noticed another person walking up the path. This time it was a woman. The looked over dressed for the occasion. She has on high heels and a sparkling cocktail dress. The sound her shoes made on the pavement sounded like hitting a nail with a hammer.

Once she approached the dealer Corey noticed something about her. Her teeth look bad. Straight enough but some blackened around the gum line. The transaction went the same as before. She complained about the price and the Latino responded in kind. "You know the business." She then handed over the cash and went on her way.

Corey decided to come out of the shadows and approach the Latino about selling. He thought if this did't work he could easily follow another junkie looking person out of a check cashing place. Corey walked toward the Latino. When he notices Corey approaching he reached behind his back. Corey knew

SERUM

what for. He had seen enough cop dramas on TNT to know he was going for a gun.

Corey held up his hands and said, "Whoa man! I just want to ask you a couple questions." Corey stopped walking letting the man assess him. He obviously didn't look like one of the regulars he meets at the park every night.

The Latino yelled, "What the fuck man? What do you want?" He never took his hand from behind his back.

"Like I said I just have a couple quick questions." Corey never moved or took his hands down. While the two were starring one another down Corey started to feel week in the knees.

"Well ask you fucking questions man and get the fuck out of here." He replied.

Corey took a deep breath thinking how to word it. "I just moved to the city and want to get into the business."

"Man, I could tell you're a cop." The Latino's stress was showing and Corey knew his was too as he began to sweat from the whole conversation.

"I'm not a cop I promise. I just am looking to make some cash. Retire young, you know." Corey said never blinking or talking his hands down. He did on the other hand begin walking toward the man.

"Not a cop huh? Turn around and let me grab your wallet." Corey complied thinking he was glad the big bills were in his front pocket in case he cashed with the wallet.

Taking his hand from behind his back he grabbed the wallet out of Corey's back right pants pocket. Corey turned around putting his hands down facing the man holding his wallet. The Latino opened it and smiled. "Corey Avery huh? Man, I can spot a fake ID at one hundred yards. I make them and probably made this one."

Corey thinking quickly answered, "I said I'm new to the city not new to the business. I don't use my real name."

Handing over his wallet the Latino asked, "You are a Joto, aren't you?"

Corey answered, "I don't know what that is."

"A fag, you are gay. Don't try to deny it I can tell." So, Corey didn't he shook his head yes. "Ok you want to get into the business fine. I think I can help you out." The Latino took a card from his wallet and handed it over. "This is my card address and phone number. Call me Pedro. Like you I don't use my real name. Meet me at my place at noon tomorrow. My family and I are getting a fresh shipment." You can prove yourself then. Make sure you bring starter cash."

Corey took the card and stuffed it in his jeans. "I will be there."

SERUM

"Now get the fuck out of here before you scare off my business." Pedro motioned to Corey to scram, and scram he did with his heart pounding.

Walking back to his apartment Corey perspired with stress. He needed a cold shower and a cigarette even though he didn't smoke. He thought he would stop by the Liquor store on the way back and get some vodka to calm his nerves while he writes his first postcard to Mark.

5

Corey woke up in a haze from the night of vodka shots and a pizza delivery. His head hurt. He thought if he were at home he would just take some aspirin and it would be all better. He didn't think to get anything for his hangovers. Corey looked at his phone charging and noticed it was ten till eleven. He jumped out of bed and threw on some clean clothes.

He thought about shaving but it would have to wait. He hated going out shaggy. While getting dressed he looked at the button camera next to his cell phone. He decided not to put it on. He wasn't trying to write a story about getting into the drug business. He was working on catching an actor buying Heroin.

Corey stomped down the stairs stopping noticing a familiar sweet smell on floor three. It was the same smell from the Chinese restaurant he ate at yesterday. After the pause, he continued on down the stairs and out to the street.

Looking at Pedro's card he noticed he was about six blocks away and wanted to walk. The apartment building listed on the card. Was another apartment building just like his. Nothing fancy about it at all. There was no door man and there was an office in the lobby. No elevator either. The building had to be ten floors compared to his five-floor building. Lucky for him the unit number was on the second floor so he only had to walk one flight of stairs. He looked at his phone and noticed he was a bit early but decided to knock on unit two-zero-two anyway.

A beautiful woman answered the door wearing a skin-tight pleather black dress. The dress accented all of her best features. "I'm here to see Pedro." Corey said when she opened the door.

"Oh, you must be the Joto." She said opening the door letting him in. He walked in to find an apartment set up not for living but packaging and distribution of drugs. No bed no anything in the room just tables and boxes. Some women were separating pills on one table and others were weighing white powder on the others. The thing that caught Corey's

SERUM

attention quick was a sweet smell he recognized from both the Chinese restaurant and the third-floor landing in his apartment building.

Pedro immediately recognized him and come over to shake his hand. "What's up Joto?" he said while shaking his hand. He then proceeded from the hand shake to a full-on pat down. Grabbing his crotch and telling him to hold his arms out. "Sorry Joto I have to make sure you don't have a wire or a gun."

Corey thought leaving his camera at home may have just saved his life. "Nope all I have on me is the starter cash and my fake ID."

"Well here is the deal Joto. I will sell you some molly and you are going to resell it at a gay club in the city." Corey looked at him with discontent as he spoke. "The going rate is forty a pill. I will sell it to you for thirty."

Corey obviously pissed looked at him and said. "I was hoping to get into heroin not a party drug at a club. And what the hell is up with the pricing. I'm only making ten a pill."

"Look Joto, you are new here, okay? You do as you're told. You have to work your way up to the harder drugs. You want to sell heroin you have to push some club drugs first. That's how this thing works. If you don't like it there is the door." Pedro or whatever his real name was pointed to the door.

"Fine," Corey said. I brought a thousand-starter cash.

"Wow Joto you are new. Look I will cut you a deal the thousand will only buy thirty-three pills. I will give you forty for the thousand. That way you can come back tomorrow with some more cash and maybe build your bank." Corey not liking it agreed and handed over the ten one hundred dollar bills.

Pedro snapped his fingers and a woman at a table counting pills counted out forty and handed them to Pedro. Pedro then gave the bag to Corey. "Look Joto you can make six-hundred tonight tomorrow night you can bank even more if you work your way up."

Corey shook his head in agreement and walked out of the apartment. He decided to take the stash back to the apartment and try to grab a nap. He knew he had a long night ahead. To help him aid in this he decided to stop by Walgreens again and pick up some Tylenol PM, some generic aspirin, and a couple Red Bulls for when he woke up.

After he reached his apartment he decided to sit down and write out the letter to Mark for the day. He took the Tylenol and began to explain to him that everything was going well he had already bought his first stash and would work on distribution tonight. He also indicated that at this rate he could be done sooner than expected.

SERUM

Corey took a long nap and well deserved. He woke up knowing exactly what club he would hit. Ironically it is the same club at sixteen he got into with a fake ID. Corey popped open the Red Bull and guzzled a third of the can. He then opened the vodka bottle and filled the Red Bull can back up. 'Got to get ready for the club.' He thought.

He showered and picked out the best outfit from his suitcase. Pink Polo shirt and tight khaki shorts and black leather sandals. He wished he had thought to pack his Chanel Blue cologne. He would just have to make do with his fresh Irish Spring sent.

Surprisingly the club is just a few blocks down from the distribution apartment where he picked up his stash. On the way to the club he decided to stop for more Chinese food at the same place. By this time, it was eight in the evening and the Dinner rush was dying down. The restaurant to Corey's surprise was still busy. He noticed on the door going in that the kitchen stayed open twenty-four seven, three-sixty-five.

'Wow If I'm in the hankering for Chinese after the club this is the place.' He went in like before but ordered something new this time. On the dinner menu, there were several things he liked He decided to try the crab, shrimp, lobster delight. The same waitress that served him the day before at lunch, served him that night. Corey ate and enjoyed it. He then went to drain the snake before heading to the club and noticed that sick sweet smell again. He realized that Chinese food was not the only thing being cooked in that kitchen. 'This must be why they are open all night.'

Corey made it to the club a little past nine. He was early and knew it. He had had plenty of rest and the Red Bull and tea were kicking in now. He wasn't even carded at the door because he was so early. They hadn't even set up to charge a cover. Then Corey realized it was not Friday or Saturday and that the club may not be as packed as one of the weekend days.

Corey went to the bar to find a fairly attractive woman with spiked hair. She had multiple piercings in her ears and one in her nose. When she stepped in front of him he noticed her hair had blue highlights. "What will you have babe?"

"For now, I will have a scotch and soda." Corey said while looking around the place. "Hopeful y it will get busier later."

She returned with a short drink that he could tell had very little soda and a ton of scotch. "Honey we just opened the doors at nine. The people you see in here now are with the entertainers."

"Entertainers?" He asked.

"Wow have you never been here before? We have a nightly drag show. Tonight, we also have some

SERUM

go-go dancers going to be on the bars. It should start getting packed around midnight when the show starts. We are even setting up private tents for the go-go boys to do private shows."

Sipping on the scotch he said, "Wow I came on the right night. Can I open a tab?"

"Sure, I just need an ID or a card."

Corey took his ID out of his wallet and handed it over. This whole go-go thing gave him a brilliant idea. He would get with the dancers before they went on stage. Tell them that he has some molly and explain how it would make them tons of money. All he had to do was sell the angle. Tell them to offer it to the Johns and sell it for fifty or sixty and just bring him forty a pill.

The Idea worked better than expected. Most of the young guys jumped on board almost immediately and the rest followed one they saw the response. Corey made his sixteen hundred and could have made more because the dancers ran out by one AM. Corey stayed around and had fun watching the drag show. He paid his eighty-dollar tab and went home around four.

CHAPTER 6

SERUM

Friday came as it usually does at the end of a long work week. For Lacy she had some work planned for Saturday and Mark would have to tag along. She would be telling him at their usual Friday lunch routine.

Today they would meet at the Ritz Carlton. This was one of Lacy's favorite lunch spots. It was just her style. The ambiance is that of a well-furnished palace. Rich wood paneling, gilded trimmings, and fabulous artwork. This was why she had gone all the way with medical school, so that she could afford nice places like this.

Once Lacy arrived she headed to the dining room. She had to first pause and take in a painting of a European scene. She was a few minutes late as usual and Mark had already been seated with an alcoholic drink on the table. From across the dining room it looked like scotch. This surprised her because he was an extreme cheapskate. He will usually just order water.

After reaching the table she said, "Wow that's not like you. Alcohol on a work day."

Mark picked up the glass and said, "I felt like splurging today. That's why I picked one of your favorite places."

"Well I have some things to talk to you about. First thing's first have you heard from Corey? I have been worried about him." She looked around looking to grab the attention of a server so that she could order her drink. She thought, 'if Mark can have a drink so should I.'

"Well Because of the postal system I have only gotten two postcards from him." Mark said taking a sip of his drink.

The waiter approached the two and asked, "Miss, what can I get you to drink?"

"I will have a vodka tonic, Chopin if you have it." She said looking back at Mark.

Stunned by this he asked, "What's gotten in to you? Drinking then going back to work?"

She said, "You can't have all the fun. Now tell me what is happening with Corey."

"Oh yeah," he said. "The two postcards. The first one was short and sweet. He went shopping for all the things he needed, and I quote, for his "shithole" of an apartment. Then the second one was promising. He said he had already infiltrated the drug dealers and had his first assignment. He said that he could be home sooner than expected if he played his cards right."

Mark looked up as the waiter come by with Lacy's drink and said, "I'll take another too please." Holding up a half empty whisky glass.

"Damn Mark slow down it's twelve in the afternoon. We haven't even ordered food yet." Lacy

SERUM

said while squeezing a lime into her drink and stirring it.

Looking over the menu Mark said. "Look Lacy I am letting my hair down. I have never lived on my own. I have always had someone in the house with me. Maybe this time apart will be good for us."

"Yeah, as long as you don't get depressed. This is only temporary he will be back soon." Lacy said while looking at the salad choices. 'Why get a salad if I am drinking?'

"I'm not worried about depression. I am enjoying myself. I'm not using a coaster. I am leaving dirty clothes on the bathroom floor. This is great! Although I have found myself googling adoption agencies in the city. I have come to the realization that it is time I give in. He is my legal husband."

"That's awesome Mark. I can't wait to be an Aunt." She said putting down the menu to show genuine interest.

"Yeah, this distance is great but makes me realize how strong the relationship really is, you know?" Mark had decided what he wanted so he sat the menu on the edge of the table as to signal the waiter back.

"Well for the strong relationship thing. You know how I am, Lacy. I have commitment-a-phobia. You know how crazy the divorce was for me. I haven't even seen anyone since." As she spoke Marks jaw dropped to the point she thought it would fall off.

"Honey that's crazy. We have to get you laid." He said with a grin and a sip of his scotch.

The waiter stopped by to see if they were ready to order. Mark ordered a rare steak and Lacy had the swordfish steak. After the waiter left, Lacy spoke up about the real questions she wanted to ask. "Mark its time. I need your help."

"Ok what do you need my help with. I'm free all weekend. You are not moving, again are you?" He asked with a frown.

"No silly. What we were talking about on Sunday." She said with a tilted head trying not to have to say the thing out loud.

"No... Absolutely not... I cannot deal with this right now. I am already worried about Corey I can't worry about you too." Finishing off the first drink with a gulp and taking a good sip of the next.

"Corey is going to be fine. He can be butch when he needs to be. For me I have been working this out all week. I have the virus. I have duplicated it and have made several different strains of the serum."

She was interrupted by Mark saying, "No... Absolutely not. We just need to have a slumber party and watch a marathon of 'The Golden Girls' on Apple TV."

"Look Mark I am not asking your permission here. I have this all laid out. I even have a body. This

SERUM

weekend is Labor Day Weekend. The office will be empty. I will have the place to myself. The stiff I can identify, but don't know who shot him. After the autopsy, he is to be cremated as per his family's wish. The timing could not be more perfect."

"For you maybe but not me." Mark raised his voice and attracted some stairs from the other patrons of the Ritz.

Lacy said, "Mark, keep your voice down. I don't need people knowing our business. You are my friend are you not, my best friend?" Mark shook his head yes reluctantly. "I need you. You said you wanted to be there. I was counting on it. I need someone else there if something goes wrong."

Whispering this time Mark said, "I will tell you what could go wrong. You could actually go through with it. Are you trying to play God?"

The mere mention of this sparked a fuse in the red head that everyone present could see even the waiter bringing plates. "I will have you know this is about more than a damn God complex. This is about catching someone before they do it again. No one should get away with murder. Now I know you are a great attorney but you have to understand something. I have a problem with someone killing and not being caught. It picks at every fiber of my being. You know that!" She took a big drink of her vodka.

Mark did know why this was such an issue for her. He remembered holding her hand at her father s funeral. They had just graduated college. One bound for medical school and one for law school. They would forever remain friends because they were there for one another when times got tough. 'Her father,' he thought. 'The day he retired went to file social security and was shot. Shot for the fifty dollars in his wallet.'

"Okay… I will be there. Don't make it too early. I plan on getting smashed tonight. It needs to be after noon." Mark polished off the scotch and raised his hand for the waiter to come back by.

"Good I need someone to be there with me. I don't know what I would do if I had to do this by myself. Don't get me wrong. I would do it by myself. I would just rather my best friend is there."

"I will do this for you. I will do this because I know one day in my life I will have to ask you to do something you are unwilling to do. You will have to do it. No questions asked. You know, that, right? No questions asked!" He waived again for someone. He needed another drink.

She shook her head in agreement. "I understand, I just need you there. For moral support if nothing else."

The two finished their meal in utter silence. They both drank heavily because both were nervous as hell about tomorrow.

SERUM
2

Mark awoke Saturday morning with one hell of a hangover. He went to the medicine cabinet for some aspirin. Thinking of how much of a dreadful day this was about to be. He wanted to call Lacy up and tell her 'Fuck it! Do it yourself.' Instead he knew he needed to be there for her. She was nervous, he could tell at the lunch the day before.

He went to the kitchen and made some coffee. 'Maybe the caffeine will help with this headache.' Mark splashed some cream in the coffee mug and poured the coffee on top. He drank a nice sip of scalding hot coffee to wash down the two aspirin. Walking into the living room he passed by the bar and poured some scotch in his coffee to top it all off. 'A little hair off the dog that bit me never hurt.'

Sitting on the sofa he gets a text from Lacy saying, don't forget about me. He hadn't forgotten. He is forcing himself to do this just as he needed to force himself off the sofa to get a shower. Time was ticking away and he didn't need to be too late.

After showering and dressing, Mark had one more cup of coffee and scotch. He made a to-go mug of coffee and a lot of scotch. He thought about taking a flask but knew he might need to be slightly sober for the day's events.

After arriving at the morgue, he started to get a sick feeling in his stomach. He paid the cab driver and got out. Standing outside the city morgue he thought to himself. 'What are you getting yourself into man? Corey would be shitting himself laughing at me right now.' He stood outside the door staring at the plaque that had Lacy's name engraved on it. After five minutes, he decided he needed to go in and get this over with.

He walked through the door and past the empty reception desk. He thought, 'Why would a morgue need a reception desk?' He walked down the hall where Lacy's office was. She was sitting at her desk the door was open. "I'm here as promised." The sick feeling intensified.

"Thank you, Mark. To tell you the truth I don't know if I could do this without you. This is groundbreaking stuff."

"Lacy, I'm pretty sure this is also illegal stuff. If not by man's law, by the law of nature. I just have to say one thing before you start." Mark held up his hand to stop her from interrupting. "I know this will make no difference to you but you need to hear it. This is wrong on so many levels. If you find out what happened to the man you will never be able present it in court. The person who did this to this man will still get away."

89

SERUM

Lacy said, "I understand all this. I still need to do this."

"Okay then let's get this over with." Mark waved his hand to the door like lead the way.

She walked down the hall to an elevator. As she pressed the button to go down she said, "You can still back out you know."

His eyes never making contact with hers, he said, "I have come this far and I have a little liquid courage with me." He held up his green coffee container.

As they boarded the elevator she said, "I wish I had thought of that." She pressed the down button. As they traveled down the one floor to the basement Mark silently shoved the green mug in her face. She grabbed it and took a big swig. "Ewe coffee and scotch what a combination."

Mark just chuckled as they hopped off the elevator. The basement was dark and slightly damp feeling. It was cool too. He thought the air must be set on sixty degrees. They walked down the long hall passing rooms labeled, Autopsy Room A, Autopsy Room B, and so on. They came to a door that said Pathology lab.

"Here we go," Lacy said as she swiped her badge on a reader next to the door handle. When they walked in Mark expected there to be a dead body on the table and all sorts of torture equipment lying around, but no. They had walked into an actual lab.

Lacy walked over to a work station with a computer. She grabbed her white lab coat off of the back of the chair. "This is my private lab," she said while putting the coat on.

"I should have worn a coat, it is chilly down here. Also, it's a bit creepy." Mark said.

"I have some extra lab coats in that closet over there. I'm sure one will fit you." She pointed to the door next to one marked restroom.

Mark found a coat and put it on. He turned to notice Lacy in a refrigerator of sorts. There were several vials of liquid all Marked with a number. She opened her notebook and picked out a vial that was glowing with a bright yellow color. It looked like she opened a bright yellow glow stick and poured it in the container.

"What's that?" Mark asked.

She responded while taking a glass out of the fridge and metal syringe out of the drawer. "This is what I call serum one-o-one. I have made several strains of this using the virus from spinal fluid. Each one is either genetically alter with or is mixed with a different radioactive isotope."

Mark cocked his head saying. "Yeah okay, if you say so. I will just stick to law."

SERUM

Lacy put the heavy-duty syringe into the vial of glowing liquid. She tilted the vial to get as much out as possible and fill the syringe. She placed the syringe on a stainless-steel instrument tray which reflected and intensified the glow of the syringe contents.

"Do you want to be in the room with me or do you just want to hang out in here?" Lacy said while getting a couple pair of purple gloves out of a dispenser.

"I have not come this far too just set in a lab with crazy radioactive shit. I am going with you. Plus, you better not leave me alone in this place." Mark uncrossed his arms and took a large sip of his scotch flavored coffee.

"Okay let's go." She opened the lab door and back to the damp dark hallway they went. The tray with the syringe lit the space they were in like candle light. They both walked without speaking to the end of the hall. There were two large metal doors Marked Morgue.

Lacy swiped her card at the reader and opened the left door, holding it open for Mark. Once inside Mark shivered. Not because of the chill in the room but because of the ambiance. The room was damp and cold. It was large with tile floors and tile walls. An avocado green color for the walls. The Wall with the cooler was what Mark had expected in a Morgue. The wall had a couple dozen cooler doors stacked three high. Some had number written on them with Dry Erase Marker, some were clean.

"Wow this is creepy Lacy." Mark said while evaluating the room. "Are we going to do this in here?"

"I would prefer we do. We have more room in here." She said while setting the instrument tray on the stand next to the examination table. "Plus, I don't want any video record of us moving the body."

Mark knocked off the rest of his scotch and coffee. He sat the traveler's mug next to the sink. He noticed things setting next to the sink that made his stomach cramp. Their next to the sink were tools and instruments of torture. 'Thank God they are dead when she uses these.' He thought watching Lacy walk to the cooler doors. Her stilettos making a clacking noise as she walked.

"I'm going to need your help here so I don't have to fetch a gurney." She opened one of the doors on the bottom row. Mark made a groaning noise as he walked over. She wasn't sure if that was from his stomach or his throat. She slid the cooler tray out revealing a dark blue body bag. The bag was fitted with three handles on each side.

"See normally I would have to load him on my own. It's a good thing you are here so I can just move him quickly." She grabbed the handle at the shoulder

SERUM

area and the one next to the middle of the bag. Mark followed her lead and grabbed the same.

Marks stomach rumbled as she said, "On three. One... Two... Three..." They together picked up the hundred and fifty or so pound bag. As the bag came off the table the leg portion of the body slumped and hovered just above the pull-out tray.

As they walked the body to the table as the bag made crackling noises. They had to slide the bag on the table so that the leg portion would slide in place. Once positioned Dr. Miller flipped on the bright halogen exam lights. She popped on the pair of fresh gloves that she retrieved from the lab. Mark just stood next to the bag watching her. She unzipped the bag from head to toe and exposed the body.

"I think I am going to be sick." Mark put his hand over his mouth then back down quickly realizing he had just touched a body bag. "Lacy, where is the man's clothes? Why is he naked? I can see everything."

Lacy cocked her head and said, "Mark grow up. He is dead. He has to have an autopsy. They remove his clothes at the hospital for processing by the crime lab."

"It's just that I have never seen a dead naked man before." He said backing away from the table.

Lacy thought, 'I see hundreds each week.' She grabbed a cloth and covered up the genitals of the corpse. "Is that better Mark? Can you stand to be in the same room now?" He nodded in agreement.

He moved closer looking the body up and down. "He was youngish, maybe in his twenties." Mark looked at the three gunshot wounds in his chest. Not like anything he had ever seen in a court room. The entry point didn't have a drop of blood. "He must have been cleaned up a little." Lacy nodded. Mark was surprised at the fact the body   had no bad odor.

Lacy replied. "I think he is a little older but I will know for sure when I do the full autopsy." She rolled the body bag down and worked it out from underneath the man.

"What are we going to do? You are not going to do the full autopsy, are you?" Mark started to step back again as if to avoid contact with the body.

She replied, "Nooo... I just want you here just in case. I'm nervous enough as it is. I don't want to do the full autopsy now. I can come back later to finish up." She   picked up the yellow heavy glowing syringe. "I just have three places I need to inject some of the virus. Put on some gloves so you can help me."

Mark did as he was told and put the purple exam gloves on without haste. He walked over and stood next to her. "What do you need me to do?" He said.

95

SERUM

"I need you to hold his head forward so that I can inject this in his brain stem." She lifted the head of John Doe number one.

"You have to be kidding me. I have to touch him?" He crossed his arms as he spoke.

"Just hold his head for me." She said while holding his head in one hand and the syringe in the other.

Mark grabbed the cranium with both hands squinting his eyes trying not to look at what she was about to do. The head was heavy to him. The corpse was not helping him any. The muscles were completely relaxed.

Mark felt the jab of the needle as Lacy plunged it into the base of the head. He looked momentarily and instantly regretted it as she was pushing through bone and cartilage making a crunching noise. He could feel the reverberations of it in his hands. Marks stomach grumbled again.

"Now lay his head down gently please." Lacy said placing the syringe on the instrument tray.

"Now what?" Mark asked taking a step back.

"Now we wait. If there is nothing in the next five minutes, we will make another injection in a different location. I don't want to overdo it all at once."

Mark nodded to this and said, "While you wait I have to go empty my bowels. This whole thing has my stomach doing flips."

Lacy took her ID card from her pocket and gave it to him. "You will need this to get back in." She said with a smirk on her face. Mark grabbed the card from her and darted to the door.

While she waited for his return she kept her eyes on the body. She thought 'I need to get the potassium ready if something goes wrong.' She walked to the supply drawer and retrieved a pre-filled potassium. She brought the lighter duty syringe and placed it next to the glowing heavy duty one.

Mark came back half expecting to see a reanimated corpse. The body was as cold and in the same position as before. "What did I Miss?" He asked.

"Nothing," she said with a sigh. "I think I will have to move on to a second injection sight. This one is either taking too long or is not the right place. I will move on to the front of the brain."

"What! How the hell are you going to access the front? Drill a hole in his head? Mark went over and got another pair of purple gloves from the box on the counter.

No silly. I will go through the eye socket." She said picking up the glowing syringe.

"I think I am going to be sick." Mark said popping the latex gloves on his hands.

SERUM

"Stop being such a baby." She said while lifting the eyelid of the corpses left eye. She positioned the needle of the syringe just over the eye and inserted it slowly. As she injected the yellow glowing substance some oozed out around the eye. She moved around the table looking at Mark never taking his hands off from in front of his mouth. On the other side of the table she did the same thing to the right eye. This time there was more oozing of the glowing yellow liquid.

Mark began to dry heave as she shut the lid on the second eye. "How long is this going to take?" He asked.

"I don't know Mark I have never reanimated the head of a corpse before." She said in the most sarcastic tone she could muster. "I will give it another five minutes before I try the next location."

"I dare not ask where the next location is." Mark's stomach was still doing flips even though there was nothing in it.

The two just starred at the corpse letting the time tick by. Nothing was happening. Lacy kept looking at the clock on the wall next to the door. As the time passed they both starred at the face of the corpse. Suddenly without warning the left hand jerked upward and slammed back on the table.

Mark looked at Lacy and said, "What the hell. I thought this was only for the head."

Lacy trying not to look worried said, "Some corpses make involuntary movements. It's normal. Some corpses even fart."

"For some reason, I don't feel any better Lacy. What if he hops off the table and runs off?" Mark said crossing his arms.

"Mark that just impossible." She said.

Mark responded, "So is reanimating a head. The truth is you don't know what's about to happen."

"Let's give it a few more minutes and see if anything more happens. If I need to I have the potassium to kill the brain." She looked at Mark trying to be reassuring but the truth is she knew that the time for involuntary movements had passed. The body had been here nearly a week.

After a good ten minutes had passed Lacy decided it was time to inject the last of serum one-zero-one. She walked over to the supply cabinet and brought out something that resembled forceps.

"What are you going... Never mind I don't want to know." Mark covered his face as lacy approached the body. Looking through his fingers he watched as she inserted the forceps in the corpse's mouth. She pried it open and leaned the head as far back as she could.

Lacy holding the forceps with one hand held the syringe in the other hand. She placed the needle

SERUM

into the upper part of the mouth and gave a forceful push with the syringe. Mark heard the cracking of more cartilage and soft tissue; again, making him dry heaves. Lacy finished off the rest of the syringe and closed the corpse's mouth back up.

"Now for more waiting." She said.

They both watched the body. At first nothing. Then came some facial twitching. The jaw of the corpse began to clench making a loud clicking noise with the teeth. The head began to trash from side to side.

Lacy and Mark embraced as they were too scared to move. They both watched in horror as the thrashing of the neck began to go faster and faster. The eyes opened glowing and oozing with the bright yellow serum. Once the body locked eyes with the two standing back watching in horror it stopped thrashing. It opened its mouth and let out a loud shrill not like any noise a human should be capable of making.

The squalling shrill was so loud that they left each other's embrace to cover their ears. The body then began to convulse and hair began to fall from the middle-aged corpses head. The full head of hair in moments was gone leaving a balled convulsing corpse with eyes wide open.

"I need to stop this." Lacy said taking her hands off her ears running for the potassium syringe. She picked it up as the corpse let out an even louder squall. This time louder and higher pitched than before. She jammed the needle into the eye socket of the corpse, (not being careful to Miss the actual eye). The eye oozed white and yellow glowing puss.

After injecting the potassium, the squalling slowly died off and the body came to rest as the limbs drew in like he was in the fetal position, but on his back. The skin of the corpse quickly changed to a jaundice look with a yellowish tinge.

Lacy looked at Mark and said "Let's get the fuck out of here. I need a drink."

Mark shook his head in agreement. "What do we do about him?"

"I will come back after lunch and take care of him. It's not like he is going anywhere. Just in case the place will be locked down."

3

On Sunday, the two meet as usual for their lunch. Mark was wearing sunglasses in the restaurant from the hangover resulting from the day before.

Lacy took a seat as Mark said, "You can never do that again. Do you understand? What happened yesterday was wrong on so many levels."

SERUM

The waiter approached for the drink order. They both ordered scotch.

"I know. When I went back last night the body was in sad shape. I didn't do an autopsy. I closed the case and sealed the body in a bag for the crematorium. I couldn't cut into it. I even notated to burn the bag for possible biohazard concerns. I had to break the arms and legs to get the limbs to lay flat."

The waiter brought the scotch and said he would be back for the order.

"Lacy I know you have more versions of the serum you want to try, but you can't. It defies nature and natural law." Mark extended his hand across the table to meet hers. She grabbed it and shook her head in agreement.

CHAPTER 7

SERUM

Corey woke up Monday morning in a bit of a haze. He looked around his tiny one room apartment and sighed. He realized it had been one week in this hell hole. He sat up he quickly looked at his burner phone to see what time it was. He didn't want to be late for his pickup.

It was a little after eleven and he had to be at the pickup apartment at one. It was time to get up and get going. If he hurried he could stop off at Starbucks and get a Grande late before he got there.

One week in, Corey had turned the three grand starter cash into over ten grand. He of course used some of the cash for personal things like meals and Starbucks; not to mention the alcohol at the clubs. Corey paid this week's rent on Friday just as planned. He was amassing a certain amount of wealth from selling ex.

Of course, human nature set in and Corey decided he would be taking some of the cash back with him when he leaves. He decided he would tell the paper he only made about ten grand and anything over that he would pocket. He had even gone so far as putting some cash aside in his kitchen drawer to deposit in his and Mikes joint account at Bank of America.

After he got up and got going he showered, shaved, and dressed. He put one hundred, one hundred dollar bills in the front pocket of his jeans. He also had a couple hundreds and some twenties in his wallet.

On the way, out the door he grabbed a cloth sack with a weeks' worth of laundry in it and jotted down the stairs. The sack reeked of cigarette smoke. He himself didn't smoke but about ninety percent of the clubs did.

On the ground floor, he meets Mr. Bill opening up the office after his lunch break. "Hey there Charlie how, are you making out?"

Corey ignoring the mix-up in names said, "Great!" He sat down the load of laundry and walked over to Bill. "This place is actually better than I could have asked for."

Bill opening the door to the office said, "Have you been able to find a job yet?"

"Oh yes. I'm working at a Chinese restaurant up the road. It's a great little place open all night. I make plenty of money there. I am even working on a little nest egg."

Standing outside the office door Bill said, "Watch who you tell that to here in this neighborhood son. People like to break in and go looking for nest eggs if you know what I mean."

This made Corey pause and think for a moment. He had almost all of his cash on him and only a couple hundred up in the apartment. He would have to risk it. After all he had most of the cash on

SERUM

him. He decided to reply with, "Oh... Ha-ha the nest egg is in the bank. I would not keep cash on me unless I was going to pay for something right then."

"Good. You seem like a good kid. Get out of this neighborhood as soon as you are able. You know the old saying, *you go to the barber shop long enough, you'll end up with a haircut.*" Bill with that nodded and walked on in the office saying, "Enjoy the rest of you day son."

Corey went over and picked up his load of laundry and walked out the front of the building. Thinking as he went, 'What the hell did Bill mean about the haircut? Was he referring to the prostitution or the drug business here? Either way I am only planning on being here a couple more weeks.'

He walked on down the street passing his fake job at the Chinese restaurant. In this area, there were several Chinese owned establishments. The one he was headed to was called *Lucky Wash and Fold.* He passed by the place many times reading the sign saying buy a laundry bag and get unlimited washes for ten dollars a bag. He thought they meant it to sound more appealing but was lost in translation.

As he walked in he was greeted by an elderly oriental woman with beautiful white hair pulled into a bun. She was wearing a tomato pin cushion on her wrist. She hobbled like she had a bum leg from around the counter. "Welcome to Lucky. How can I help?"

"I would like to use your wash and fold service. I bout this bag a couple days ago and wanted to use the promotion." Corey picked up the oversized bag for her to see.

"Ok.. Ok.. I will give you ten-dollar service. No press?" She said while writing out a ticket from her apron.

"No none of it is dressy. Just the wash and fold is fine." He put the bag on the counter pulling on the draw string to keep it closed.

"Ok good..." She said while finishing up the ticket. She ripped the bottom of the ticket off. "Bring this tomorrow and pay then. I will take good care for you." She put her end of the ticket on the drawstring on the bag via Denison gun.

Corey said, "Thanks." He turned and walked out the front door. Now he was off to Starbucks with thirty minutes to spare. The great thing about the city was there was a Starbucks on every corner and the smallest coffee there is a tall. He always got the same thing. A white mocha.

After the coffee run he was off to the pickup location. On the way down the street he noticed two children outside of their apartment building having the time of their lives with sidewalk chalk and a jump rope. He thought, 'This is how you should grow up. Not with your face in front of a screen but outside

SERUM

using your imagination. These kids are in the part of town where there is probably no cable or internet for them anyway.'

Corey made it to the rundown building where his pickup apartment was. He was slightly early, but decided to go up anyway. As he made it to the apartment a black man was coming out of the apartment he was about to enter. He had a duffle bag. 'This is probably a big take for him.' Corey thought as he walked through the open door, closing it behind him.

Pedro immediately recognized him and said. "Joto you know we have scheduled pickup times for a reason. You can't be early and you can't be late. What If we were not finished with the man before you? He might have shot your ass for barging through the door."

Corey looking at a loss for words and a little shocked replied, "Sorry I didn't think about it I guess." Corey then pulled the ten grand from his pocket. "Look, when can I graduate to something bigger? This whole gay club thing is nice but I want to be in a larger business. I have ten K today. What can you do for me?"

Pedro and the other women working at the tables stopped and looked at one another. Pedro said, "What do you want to sell?"

Corey said, "Heroin."

"Look Joto I get it you want to make some big cash fast. You need more than ten K to start in on this business. I will, on the other hand, let you try your hand at some Meth."

"Meth?" Corey said disappointed.

"Yeah Meth, in this city, is the poor man's drug. You don't need to have syringes or anything. Just snort or eat it. I will give you a supply for the ten K and send you to tent city tonight to sell it." Pedro held out his hand for the stack of bills. He handed them over to a beautiful Latino woman who placed them in a bank counting machine.

"Ok fine. If I do this this week can I move up to Heroin next week?" Corey said while he watched the ladies scrabbling to put together his order.

"Boy you are one brave Joto that's for sure. If you work tent city this week I will send you up town next. You will have enough by then." One of the well-dressed women handed over a large manila package of individually packaged gram bags. "This is fu l of five hundred baggies. One gram each. You don't need to go over fifty bucks a gram. There will be competition there. I would say start at forty and move down five bucks or more for bulk purchases. You have the ones who like to buy ten or twenty packs to sell once the others deplete their stash.

SERUM

Core looked at the manila package and took it under his arm. "So where is this tent city, and why do you call it that?"

"Boy you are new to this whole thing, aren't you?" He wrote an address on an index card while talking. "The tent city is where the homeless people live. They all live in a tent or cardboard box or something like that."

Pedro handed over the index card and said, "This is where you need to go. It is at the edge of the city. It's a Family Dollar. You will go directly behind the Family Dollar and up the hill into the woods. That's where you will find the city you need to sell to."

Corey took the card. "How do I advertise that I am selling?"

Chuckling, Pedro looked at the women in the room. "Look Joto you will be the best dressed out there. I think you will even have a leg up on the other dealers. They will know and come to you I am certain. As soon as they establish you are not a cop."

Corey looking at the card realized he would have to take a cab, that this was just not a trip he needed to walk. "Ok I will do this but I want to move to the good stuff soon."

"Boy you got some gumption Joto. Now get the fuck out of here before the next person arrives.

Next time don't be early." Pedro waved his hand in a dismissive sort of way.

Corey did what he was told and left as he was walking down to the street he glanced at a person entering the building with a duffle bag. He knew instantly that he was there to get his pickup. It was alarming to Corey that he was able to identify the other dealers on sight now. Had he already infiltrated the whole industry in one week?

After leaving the building the envelope tucked under his arm and the index card in his hand he headed to his fake place of employment for some Chinese Food. He decided that after he ate he would wait a period of time before heading to the Family Dollar. He wanted to get there just before dark.

2

Lacy started her Monday like any other. She got up, had some coffee and showered. She was still running over the events of the day before in her mind. She had somewhat done what she had set out to do. She had reanimated a corpse. Of course, it didn't go as planned.

Mark advised her to destroy the vials of experimental serums. Lacy had no such intent. She knew what to expect now. 'There was no reason to

SERUM

give up because Mark doesn't have the stomach for it,' she thought.

Lacy got dressed in one of her favorite Versace red skinny dresses. She also popped on some Christian Louboutin black shoes with the red souls to match the dress. Needless to say, she felt good. She picked up her iPhone and began to read her emails as she filled a to-go coffee container.

It looked like she had nothing pressing on her schedule for the day. She had one autopsy of an elderly gentlemen who apparently had a stroke. Unless she was called out on some case she would just be at the office doing paperwork. Maybe she would do some research as to what went wrong on her first trial.

Leaving the building she gave her door man a five-dollar bill to fetch her a cab while she finished up her emails on her phone. She shot a text to Mark asking if he was ok and if he needed to talk. She knew he would need too.

As she stepped into the cab she sighed as she gave the address to the city morgue. She slid the iPhone in her purse as the cab driver began to talk. "So, I think I have seen you somewhere before. You are that crime lady right?" The elderly driver asked.

"I'm the city medical examiner. I do investigate crimes with the police department." Lacy spoke not taking her eyes off the rear-view mirror they were communicating through. She noticed his taxi permit hanging from the mirror. *Marty Ginsberg* it said.

"Wow that must be an exciting job..." She nodded to his statement thinking she would just appease him until she made it to the office. ' Say... Did you ever find out what happened to that stabbing shooting thing a couple weeks ago?"

She looked at her shoes as he asked. "No, we are still investigating it. The police have leads and hopefully we can close it soon." She said this knowing very well that the case was dead. There was no new evidence and no new anything. The bodies were just gone. There is nothing more she could do. If only she had the right serum for that case she could say she did everything possible.

"Here we are Miss, its fifteen fitty. Cash or charge?" He asked with a half toothless grin.

She pulled a twenty from her purse and said, "Keep the change Marty."

He looked shocked as he took the change from her. "You know my name?" She pointed to the taxi permit on the rear-view mirror as she snapped her purse closed. "Wow you are good lady. I know you will solve the murders. You have what it takes." Marty tipped his hat and said, "Morning Miss" as she stepped out of the cab.

As she walked to the door she thought, 'I have what it takes. He is right; I do have what it takes. I had

SERUM

one bad experiment.' She opened the front door acknowledging the receptionist Doris. Or was it Dorothy? She never was good at all the names. "I am a scientist. I don't give up because something doesn't work the first go round. That why I made so many strains of this.' She walked down the hall to her office with her Christian Louboutin's clacking the whole way.

She shut the door and sat at the sofa across from her desk. 'I can't give up now. There are too many unsolved murders. I did not seek office and win to let the same number of unsolved cases pass by.' Her pep-talk to herself was building momentum. 'I just wish the man on my table today was not a stroke victim. I can't risk the brain trauma interfering with the outcome of the test.

She jumped off the sofa and darted for her desk. 'I wonder if someone else has a case I can steal.' She jiggled the mouse on her computer waiting on it to wake up. She peered through the schedule for the building. There was nothing that would do any good. Car crash and natural causes. Nothing labeled foul play or suspicious.

She sat back in her chair and thought, 'I can't give up I don't have to involve Mark but I can't give up.'

As she completed the thought her iPhone made a dinging noise. Mark had text her back. 'Let's do Lunch'

3

After writing his daily postcard to Mark, Corey began to get ready to head to the Family Dollar. He decided to take a messenger bag. This would make things easier and less conspicuous. He could keep the gram baggies in one side and the cash in the other.

Corey left the building passing one of his neighbors on the way down. This was the first time he had seen a neighbor since he had moved in. She was an older woman caring a brown grocery bag. Her hair was so white and soft looking. If he had to guess she was in her eighties. He nodded as he passed her, and she didn't acknowledge him.

Corey went on out of the building and walked toward the nearest Starbucks. He decided he would grab a latte then catch a cab to the Family Dollar up town.

At Starbucks, he ordered and remembered he had put his wallet in the messenger bag as he went to pay. As nonchalantly as possible he opened the bags flap trying not to reveal the front compartment with baggies of Meth. He was certain the Barista was on to him as he dropped one of the small bags to the floor

SERUM

as he took out his wallet. Before paying he bent down and scooped up the blue baggie filled with white powder. He gave her a five and put the change in her tip jar. Embarrassed he almost left without the latte.

Once outside he hailed the nearest cab and gave the driver the address. The driver looked at Corey with a surprised look on his face and said, "Are you sure you want to go there? There are several nicer Family Dollar stores closer." Corey just nodded his head.

Once in the parking lot Corey handed over thirty-five dollars and stepped out of the cab. He patted his leather messenger bag as he looked at the front facade of the worn-down Family Dollar. Even the quarter operated riding games outside were run down. The race car's paint was flacking off and was missing its steering wheel. The rocket ship on the other side of the door was in sad shape too with the tip broken off and exposed wires at the base.

Corey finished off his coffee and tossed the cup at an overflowing trash can next to the entrance. He paused and tried to collect his thoughts. He was almost preparing himself for what he was about to walk into. Corey walked to the edge of the Family Dollar and the strip shopping center. He looked around the corner of the building where a delivery truck was coming from behind the building.

One the truck passed Corey noticed a clear pathway in the dirt behind the dumpsters it was well traveled and cut straight through the row of pine trees into the wooded area. He instantly knew that was the entrance of Tent City. He walked toward the tree line looking over his shoulder trying to see if anyone was watching him.

As Corey walked up the steep incline passing the thick patch of pine trees he felt a knot forming in his stomach. He felt sick at the thought of feeding drugs to the homeless. He had not thought about it like this before, but he was perpetuating the stereotype. Trying to suppress his feelings he walked on through the trees until he came to the top of the hill.

As Corey stood at the top of the hill he looked down into the trees. He could see the city, and a city it was. There were tarps strung up between trees. Some setups were of actual tents from an outdoors store. Some people he noticed had the old cardboard box. It all was surreal to Corey. He thought to himself, 'I bet the Family Dollar or any of the surrounding stores have no problem getting rid of the discarded boxes.

Corey stood there looking at the ecosystem. He watched the people going from tent to tent socializing. It looked like a system had formed around one large center tent. Out of the hundreds of tents in the area the one large one in the center reminded him

SERUM

of a circus tent. It was strung up made of a white cloth just like something out of Barnum and Bailey's.

As he watched wondering how in the world he would make an entrance into the tent ecosystem, he felt a tap on his right shoulder. "Your... Your.... the new guy aren't you?" The thin young man with dark hair asked.

Corey replied, "New Guy?" Shifting his weight to face the strange looking guy wearing a Zelda hoodie.

"Yeah. You... You... know... The new dealer. You are the first one here to... to... tonight." Corey nodded wondering if he should address the stammer. I... I... am Timmy by the way.

"I was told around night time but I wanted to check the place out first. I have never seen anything like it. How many people are here?" Corey looked back and forth between Timmy and the city.

"Well... Well... if you have the right stuff hundreds. I... I... Can show you around if you want?" Timmy held out his hand like he was waiting for something.

"I see." Corey said to his new guide. "You just need payment in what I am peddling right?" He reached into his bag without opening the flap all the way. He didn't want Timmy to see how much he had. Corey pulled a gram blue baggy from his messenger bag. He placed it in the palm of Timmy's hand and looked around nervously.

Timmy took the baggie opened it and dipped his finger inside. He pulled a white powder coating his index finger and rubbed it on his upper gum line. "Thanks." He said "Now let's get started. The other will be here soon and you will have a little competition to deal with."

"You didn't stammer that time." Corey observed.

"Yeah it's something to do with the drug. Once it is in my bloodstream it takes just a short time to stop the jitters and stutter" Timmy began to walk toward the tent city waving for Corey to follow.

The short walk gave Corey some time to think about the stammer. "Is that why you live here to control the stammering?"

Timmy paused and turned. "I live here by choice as do most of these people. I don't work, I don't pay taxes. Many of us don't. We live here in a community because we understand one another. Most of us like drugs. This is an easy avenue. Some people are down on their luck and just need a support system. I will walk you through and introduce you to the ones you need to deal with. After I have finished you will pay me either three hundred or a weeks' worth. Whatever you want."

SERUM

Corey paused stunned at the composure the once stammering man had giving his speech. "Sounds fine to me. Let's get the show on the road."

"Follow me and don't ask them too many questions. Got it?" Timmy turned and began walking to the tent line. Corey obeyed and followed. After all, having a guide would make this a bit easier.

As they infiltrated the city Corey noticed there was actually an organized system to the city. There were dirt roads that connected rows of tents. For being a city for the homeless it was well put together.

Timmy stopped outside of a tent made from an old tin roof piece and walls made of blue tarp. "Maud are you home?" He said sliding the tarp causing it to make a crinkling noise.

An older lady with two sweat shirts on poked her head from the tent. She looked to be in her sixties. She was malnourished and pale. It made Corey's heart skip a beat when he saw her. "Come in boys she said."

Corey followed Timmy inside ducking his head not to hit it on the tin roof. The older woman spoke with a raspy voice. "Boys sit anywhere. My tent is your tent." Corey sat on a turned over milk crate in the ten by ten space. Timmy stood as the older woman sat in a beanbag chair.

Timmy started the conversation. "Maud this is our new guy. He is early scoping out the area. He has some fresh stuff not cut with a bunch of trash."

Maud nodded her head as she spoke. "So, I can see your stammer is gone." She turned to stare into Corey's eyes. "See the new people have yet to be corrupted by the system. The older dealers like to cut the shit with baking soda and baby laxatives. What I do is I like to buy a stash and keep it on hand here in my tent. I'm not a user but when people like Timmy run out, or get some bad shit I like to have some good on hand to elevate their pain, so to speak."

"Aren't you scared of being robbed or mugged?" Corey asked.

Maud pulled a two-barrel shot gun from next to her beanbag chair. "No one fucking bit." She grinned as she patted the old Smith & Weston.

Timmy spoke up. "No one messes with Maud. She is saving for retirement, or so she says."

"The truth is Timmy I have a bank account where I put all this money I make. I have two grandchildren that have never meet me. My daughter married a hoity-toity man. When I fell on hard times she divorced me. As much as a daughter can." The woman raised her hand and paused. "Now I can't blame her. I was not a great mother and I treated her awful. These things happen to people you see. When I die I have a will with a lawyer. All my cash and this

121

SERUM

Smith & Weston will go to those two girls. In my twenty some years here I have amassed a fortune."

"Wow..." Corey said patting his bag. "To tell you the truth I am doing this so I can adopt a child. I know it sounds strange but this is the quickest way to accumulate a small fortune, you know."

"Honey I don't judge a single person. I'm just a cog in the machine. You can't get anywhere in this world without taking a risk. You and I are evidence of this. Now how many grams do you have?" Maude pointed to his messenger bag.

Corey patted his bag and said, "I have five hundred."

Maud's eyes opened big. "Five large huh? Well look I have three grand. I can take a hundred off you for that if you want?" I'm sure that's less than you had planned on selling it for but I have to turn some cash too you know. For the grandkids." She lowered her eyes trying to play on his sympathy.

"It's a deal." Corey said, "I would just as soon get rid of all this as soon as possible." Corey opened the bag and began counting out baggies.

"Young man. Let me give you some advice. I can tell you are new. Get out of this business as soon as possible and get your kid. This is not the place for you. I can look at you and tell. The others will be able to tell as well." Maud opened her leather purse next

122

to her beanbag chair and began counting one hundred dollar bills as Corey counted blue packs.

The two exchanged handfuls of currency. One of drugs and one of money. Even though Corey was only making ten bucks a pack the way he figured it was he just banked a grand off of his first transaction.

"So, I will be more prepared for next time. Will you always have this level of supplies?" Maud spoke while placing the little blue packets in her purse.

"I hope to be continuously stepping up my supply level. I hope to move on before too long. I hope not to be selling this for more than another week." Corey counted the money not for the fact that he did not trust her but it had become practice. The people at the club constantly tried to stiff him on a few bucks here and there.

"See that's good thing babe. You will flood the Market over the next week and then will vanish leaving a hole I can fill. Come back by tomorrow and let me fill up on some more before you go on your rounds. That way I can gain a supply. I will keep it all in the safe at the bank. I think J.P. Morgan himself would shit to know how many drugs and drug money ran through his bank." Maud patted her purse protecting her purchase.

Corey stood up and nodded. "I will see you tomorrow then?"

"Yeah baby you come on by. I will be here waiting." She waived her hand dissuasively. "Oh boy

SERUM

listen… You treat Timmy right you here. He is like a son to me."

Corey nodded in agreement and Timmy and he left the tent. Once outside a crowd had begun to gather. People knew why he was here now. They knew what a stranger stopping in Maud's tent meant. He had what they all wanted. He had the stuff. Corey had some desperate people swarming around him. He began filling orders without ever stepping away from Maud's tent.

Corey said to the crowd that formed, "Fifty a gram." The people then began to shovel out the cash. Some had big bills some had panhandling change. Corey relied on Timmy to count most of the change. People would hand him a hundred he would hand back two packs. Corey really didn't have to do that much work.

After he had satisfied the crowd of homeless dissidents Corey looked into his pack and still had at least two hundred packs to get rid of. He looked up at Timmy with a concerned look on his face.

"Don't… Don't… Worry, bu… bu… boss." The stutter had returned. Timmy took the blue pack from his pocket and rubbed some more of the contents on his gum line. After a couple seconds, he spoke again. "We still have a lot of ground to cover. This is a big city boss."

The two traveled through the city as darkness fell. Knocking, or as best you can on a tent, throughout the homes in the city. One after another they went from tent to tent. Some purchasing ten packs some only one some trying to trade or barter. Timmy would speak up saying, "The price is set. Boss don't need any of your goods he needs cash." For this Corey was grateful so he would not have to deal with the haggle.

After the messenger bag was empty of blue bags and full of a crazy amount of cash he looked at Timmy and said. "We are done I have no more to peddle. Do you mind if I give you some of the smaller bills?"

Timmy responded, "No sir money spends regardless."

Corey began to count out three hundred in ones and fives. He handed Timmy the wad of cash and thanked him for his services. "Timmy do you mind showing me the way back to the entrance. I think I have been turned around slightly."

Timmy pointed to the big white tent in the center of the city. "Follow me I will show you the best way to remember where you are." Corey did as Timmy said and followed him to the center tent.

Once inside the tent, Corey realized what the purpose of the tent was. It was a lot like a town center. It was almost like a Market where people were trading goods. There was a food kitchen set up where

SERUM

people were getting their nightly meals. Corey recognized Maud slapping people's plate with some mashed potatoes. She had her purse securely sung over her shoulder as she served the masses.

Timmy went to the one side of the tent. He pointed forward so that Corey could see. "There is the Family Dollar sign. See it lit up there? That's your way out."

Corey took the information and started walking. He paused a couple feet outside the tent and looked back at Timmy. He remembered he had one blue packet in his front pouch of his bag. He put it there at the coffee shop. He took it out ant turned around. He walked over to Timmy and handed it to him. "Here buddy thank you so much for your help. I look forward to seeing you tomorrow."

With that Timmy nodded and put the pack in his front pocket. Corey turned to find a large black man standing in front go him. He had a duffle bag in his hand and three other black men standing behind him.

He spoke in a coarse manner to Corey. "So, you are trying to barge in on my turf. I think we need to teach him a lesson boys." The man turned to the other men standing behind him.

They began to surround Corey. Corey had no weapon or no way out. He had no street scene, and

126

wasn't prepared to be confronted by rival drug dealers. The larger man moved in close and kneed Corey in the balls. Corey fell to the ground in agonizing pain. Another man began to kick Corey in the stomach.

While lying there taking the abuse there was an unmistakable sound. The sound of a gun. People began to scatter. The men stopped kicking and beating Corey as Maud aimed the gun at them. She had taken a revolver from her purse and had its crosshairs on the main man in the group.

"I dare you men to make another fuckin move!" Maud moved in not dropping the gun. "He is protected. You mess with him you mess with me. Now back the fuck off." The men did as she asked and walked around through the crowd to begin conducting their business.

"Get up honey, I will walk you out." Corey stood with dirt all over his clothes and blood on his lip. Maud walked with him holding him by the waist toward the Family Dollar sign.

At the clearing where the tree line meets the hill to the parking lot Maud said. "Honey get the cash you need and get the fuck out of this business. Hell... Get the fuck out of this city. You don't want to run the risk of someone recognizing you and your child walking down Maddison Avenue while they panhandle."

SERUM

Corey looked hopelessly at her and said. "I hope to only be doing this till the end of next week. I hope by then I can be done for good and cash out."

Maud took the gun from her purse and handed it to Corey. "Put this in your bag. I don't know why the hell you are selling drugs without a firearm on you. No one gave you any sense when they talked you into this."

"I have to admit I am out of my league. Thank you, but what will you do?" Corey held the gun as if it were his first time ever holding one.

"Honey there are more arms where that come from I assure you. You saw what I had next to my chair. I haven't lasted this long without learning how to protect myself. Take it. Consider it a gift." Maud pointed to the Family Dollar sign and said, "Now get!"

Corey did as he was told and got. He went to the street not being able to see Maud but knew she was still there watching until he got into a cab. Corey had the cab drop him off in the little china town so he could get some Chinese food from his fake job.

4

CHRISTOPHER MCDONALD

Tuesday morning came early for Lacy as she had a call from her old friend at the police station. William Cox had called her to inform her there had been a double homicide in the park overnight. So around six in the morning she left her home to head the short distance to Central Park. She decided to walk so that she could get some Starbucks on the way.

She made it to the park a little after six thirty as the sun was starting to shine across the morning dew. She meet Detective Cox at the police tape line as joggers and baby walkers were getting their morning started.

"What do we have here William?" She asked while ducking under the crime scene tape.

William lifted the tape to let her cross underneath. "Well the usual thing I call you for. One of your guys got the call and could not give a clear time of death or ID. So that means I call the top dog before we move the bodies."

Dr. Miller pulled some gloves from her purse while handing William her coffee cup. She also pulled some covers for her designer shoes. Prada today. She slapped on the gloves and the hairnets for her shoes then took her coffee back.

She began to circle the first body as she always did. She had to photograph every detail in her mind that she could. The first victim was laying on his back. He looked to be a black man in his thirties. She noticed the one gunshot wound to the head. Her

SERUM

instant thought given the placement of the legs and feet is that he was on his knees. "It was an execution for this one. He was on his knees begging. The shooter was standing maybe two feet away."

"Damn Lacy that was quick." Detective cox notated every detail she said in his notepad.

"Will, I thought you said there were two? Where is the other guy?" Lacy looked side to side inside the tape line.

"The other is a couple hundred yards away. He must have witnessed this execution and ran. Im sure you will agree when we get over there." They both began to walk over to the second tape line in the clearing between some trees.

As they approached Lacy noticed this was a white male, slender. He was face down but she could see bruises on his forearms as he lay with his face in the dirt. She had a thought given the man's build and physique. 'It can't be Corey.'

She charged in-front of Detective Cox and scooted under the tape line. She moved around do she could see the man's face. It wasn't Corey. She took a deep breath.

"Everything okay Doc?" William asked.

"Yeah Will. I thought it was a friend at first. You know how that initial reaction can be sometimes don't you?" She began to compose herself as Will gave her an *I guess* gesture.

She began to walk around the body looking again at every detail. The fact he still had a wrist watch but no wallet. The look of his glasses smashed into his face by the impact of the fall. She looked at the gunshot wounds. Three in the back. "He was running for his life. Given the placement of the wounds the assailant was running too. He chased him down then took his wallet."

"Why take his wallet but not the watch?" Detective Cox asked.

"He is giving himself some time. If we know who this man is he will link to the killer in some way." Dr. Miller took one more spin around the crime scene. "Bag them, guys." She said to her people from the morgue.

"Will go ahead and print them before they take them off. The sooner we can ID the one shot in the back the sooner we can find the killer." She walked back out from under the tape line.

"I want you to call me as soon as you know something Will. I will do the same. As soon as I get back I will start working on them both myself so that we can catch this person within the first forty-eight." Lacy not looking back headed straight to the street. She raised her arm as soon as she made it out of the park so that she could get to the lab as quick as possible.

SERUM

When she made it to the Morgue she went straight to her office and shut the door. She picked up the phone and called another medical examiner in the building who handled the take in of bodies. She made it clear that she was to be the one to process them.

She sat back in her chair and pondered a while. She didn't want to rush into anything. She still had the dental records and other things if the prints didn't match anything. After all, not every state prints people for DMV records. Lacy knew but didn't know at the same time that this would be her second experiment.

After thinking for a period of time she received a phone call from Detective Cox. "Lacy the prints are not in the system for the white guy but the black guy is a felon. He was upstate last week on a drug charge. Now he is on your slab. I will email you the information I have on him. Good luck with the white dude."

Lacy thanked him and hung up the phone. This was in a way good news to her. She knew she could not reanimate someone shot in the head. She could on other hand animate the, 'White Guy,' as the detective put it. Of course, she would have to do the usual things like check for dental work and the usual tattoo search etc...

Dr. Miller picked up the phone and called back to the receiving medical examiner. She called to inform him that she would take the Caucasian male that the police have identified the African American male; he could be assigned to another ME.

5

Corey started his Tuesday off the same ole way. He woke up late took a shower then off to the pickup site. Today on the other hand was a little tough getting started. He wasn't able to spring out of bed as usual like days before. He had to slowly lean up while his aching muscles sent needles down his spine. He had his first ass whooping since high-school. This time not for being gay but taking Market away from another dealer.

Corey hobbled over to the bathtub holding his arm in a hooked position. He stripped his clothes off and turned on the shower. The pipes rattled as he noticed the bruising on his stomach. He was the strangest color. He looked not black and blue but almost moss green and yellow. He thought, 'They should change that. It's nothing like black and blue.'

When he got under the water he could feel the muscles in his back relax and shoot pain up his spine. As he began to wash he noticed spots in places he didn't even remember being kicked. He wondered

SERUM

why the people at the Chinese restaurant looked so strangely when they saw him last night. He looked like shit. The dirt he washed off was spiraling down the drain. He got out of the shower and grabbed for the towel on the back of the toilet.

With a loud clank, he simultaneously dropped the gun to the floor and pulled the towel to the tub. He had forgotten in his stupor from vodka, to kill the pain, he wrapped the gun Maud had given him in a towel. Lucky the gun bounced making a clank and clack then settled without going off.

He stepped out of the bathtub and wrapped the towel around his bruised body. He reached for the bottle of Smirnoff vodka still with the top off and took a big gulp. Heaving from the burn of pure alcohol going down his throat he felt the effects almost instantly.

He put on the last clean polo shirt and khaki pants he had. This reminded him he needed to go by and pick up his laundry. He looked at his phone. He had actually given himself enough time to get some things done before going to the pickup site. He would go by and gather his clothes, get some coffee and then move to the pickup. He hadn't even counted the cash he made from the night before.

He slid flip-flops on and gathered about thirty bucks in cash from his messenger bag. He walked out of the apartment to the stairs. When he took the first step he knew that he was hurt. He didn't know how bad until he made it all the way down to the first floor. Every crippling step made him cringe.

Once outside the building Corey looked up to the warming sun. He didn't expect what happened last night. He would on the other hand be better prepared for tonight. He now had a gun and a little more awareness on his side.

Walking into the nearest Starbucks he ordered his usual latte and paid. He decided to sit on one of the plush sofas lining the wall opposite the counter. He sat there pondering if all this pain and all this was really worth it. He had come so far so fast and it looked like he could be finished with this in one month not two. His stomach grumbled.

He remembered he hadn't eaten since last night. Chinese food seem to leave the system quicker than most food. Corey stood slowly and painfully to view the pastry case. He noticed they had ham and cheese croissant. He went over and ordered the five-dollar delicacy.

After his coffee run he decided to pay his laundress a visit or he would be out of clothes by tomorrow. The block and a half back from Starbucks to pick up his clothes became easier. Passably due to the caffeine or the sandwich, but more than likely a combination of both.

SERUM

He walked in and the same elderly Chinese woman greeted him from behind the counter. He was reaching for his ticket but she already knew who he was and what bag was his. She pulled the bag from behind the counter and walked it around to Corey. "All clean for you." She said. "Ten dollaa."

Corey pulled out ten one dollar bills and placed another five dollars in her tip jar. "Thank you so much Miss," he said cringing while picking up the bag.

"Oh, you come back any time here. We do you good job." She walked back behind the counter and hit a button on the cash drawer. "You have good day." Corey nodded and hobbled out of the shop.

He made it back to the building feeling slightly better than when he left. 'I guess the more I work the soreness out the better,' he thought while walking into the building. he looked at the steps. 'Five flights. Going down was painful. Going up will be sheer agony.'

He began the track up the stairs. As he had predicted the trip hurt but not as bad as earlier. Once back to his apartment he laid back down on the bed. He thought, 'I have to work through this. I can't give up. I have come so far and sacrificed so much. I have to keep this up. I will do this and I will make sure I never take another case like this as long as I am sane.'

136

Corey set the alarm on his burner phone and stared at the celling until time for the pickup. Corey got up and got his bag. He stuffed the gun in the back of his khakis. He left to go and pick up the stuff. He figured if he made it around the same time tonight he could maybe avoid the whole ass whooping thing he had experienced the night before.

The trip down the stairs was much easier but still painful. He could almost feel his heartbeat in the bruise on his stomach. Corey left the building with his stomach hurting externally and internally. His nerves were doing cartwheels. He didn't know if he could finish out the week with rivals like he meet last night.

He arrived at the pickup location right on time and went on up to the apartment. He handed over his messenger bag and had the well-dressed woman sort and count the cash.

"Joto this is not a bank you know you could at least sort the shit for us." Pedro cocked his head while his women worked on the cash.

"Look when I was working the night club I had a way of changing out the bills with the house. Now I'm in a freaking tent city with nothing but a family dollar nearby. What do you expect me to do? Walk in to the nearest Chase branch and say give me hundreds for all this homeless people cash." Corey was beginning to get loud and frustrated as he spoke.

"Calm the fuck down Joto. We will take care of the cash. You snap on me again we will have a

SERUM

problem. Just take a seat on the sofa." He pointed to a sofa near the kitchenette. Corey did as instructed.

Pedro walked over to the fridge and took out a can of Coors Light and handed it to Corey. "I can tell Joto you just got your ass beat."

"Yeah I had no idea that I would have rivals at this place." Corey popped the top on the can with a hiss.

"You wanted to step up. This is what you have to deal with. The higher up the chain you go the more competition there is. You are not going to make it to the park with that type of expectation." Pedro looked at the woman counting the cash she nodded and handed him a piece of paper.

"You must have met the old lady last night and she must have liked you. You must remind her of someone. She usually doesn't allow you to make much profit. Not more than a buck anyway. You made enough last night to move up your supply by twenty-five percent." Pedro balled up the paper and tossed it in the bin. "We will get it ready. You just sit and drink the beer.

"How do I deal with the others?" Corey asked while taking gulps of the Coors can. "They travel in packs and had a duffle bag full of stuff."

"Your business will sell itself. They probably don't have near the quality you do. See people get greedy and cut the shit. We like to think our people come to us because of the quality." Pedro watched over the women packing up the messenger bag.

"Maud said she knew I had good stuff. How does someone know?" Corey asked

"Joto you are still new at this whole thing. Everyone can tell. You just need to make the cash you need and get the fuck out. That's my advice. You look too pure. Everyone that looks at you can see you are too honest to cut the shit or cheat someone." Pedro was passed the messenger bag by his co-worker, or whatever she was. "Joto good luck tonight and be careful."

Corey took the bag and left the apartment. He wondered why he ever took the job. Four hundred thousand. Plus, the money he will pocket from the drug sale. He has been advised to get the hell out of town.

All he knew is that he was three miles from home and home sick as fuck. He Missed Mark. He Missed dressing up and putting on a bowtie for work. He missed the lunches with Mark and Lacy. He missed Sunday Funday.

He walked down to the street, and decided to head over to the bar across the street from the apartment building where he picked up his supply. The Salty Dog the sign said on the door as he walked in. It was nothing more than a straight biker type bar. There was an electronic juke box on the wall next to

SERUM

the door as he walked in. It was playing some old
Hank Williams Jr. tune. He knew the voice but
despised the depressing music.

Corey walked in and sat at the bar. There were
three other people sitting at the bar with one asleep
in his beer. Two other people were shooting pool at
the other end of the bar. An old man with white hair
and white beard walked up to Corey puffing on a
cigarette. "What can I get yah?" The man said with a
raspy smoking voice and Brooklyn accent.

"I will take a beer." Corey said while adjusting
his bag to not fall off.

"Well buddy in case you haven't noticed, this is
a bar. We have lots of beer. What kind tickles your
fancy?" The man puffed on the cigarette and put it
out in an ash tray in front of Corey.

Not amused by the sarcasm Corey replied, "I
will just take a Bud Light draft." After a few seconds,
the bartender returned with a frosted mug of Bud.
Saying nothing the bartender started wiping the bar
down with his towel.

Corey sat pondering his future. Trying to figure
out what he would do. All he knew at this point is he
was lonely and homesick. He just wanted to sit there
at the bar drowning his sorrows until time to meet up
with Timmy and Maud.

One after another he ordered beer. Talking to the bartender he realized that he missed human connections. The bartender was rough and brass with his speech but none the less Corey loved the conversation. They talked about a range of subjects from Bipolar Disorder to alcoholism. Around five o'clock Corey paid his bar tab so that he could head to the city of tents.

After paying Corey stood up from the bar stool. He stumbled as he made it to his feet. The bartender said, "Whoo buddy you need some coffee," as he lit another cigarette. Corey figured that had to be his tenth cigarette.

Corey corrected his posture. "I'm fine. I am catching a cab."

"Yeah well you have to make it to the curb first." The bartender added as he puffed on the cigarette.

"I will be fine sir, thank you." Corey said while turning to the door. He walked out looking like he was walking a wiggly line.

Once Outside he successfully hailed a cab. He was let out at the Family Dollar like the day before. This time the driver didn't question the choice of dollar stores. Corey walked to the end of the building and around to the dumpster. He walked up the hill to find Timmy standing waiting. Corey adjusted the gun in the back of his pants.

"Ha... ha... hi boss," Timmy said.

SERUM

"How are you today?" Corey asked while taking a blue pack from his bag and handing it over to Timmy.

"Tha tha thank you." Timmy like the day before took some of the white powder and rubbed it on his gum line. After a couple of minutes, he started to sound more normal again. "Maud wants to speak with you."

"Well I knew she wanted me to stop by and give her a deal first." Core said patting Timmy on the shoulder.

"She has more than that to talk about. There is a threat on you." Timmy started walking in the direction of Maud's tent.

"Threat! What?" Corey exclaimed.

"Maud will have to explain. Let's go before it gets late." Timmy didn't stop to see if Corey was close behind. Corey at this point was in a little bit of shock. The two hurried into the tent without announcing their presence.

Maud jumped up from her bean bag chair with the rifle in her arms. "Dear boy, sit please. We have much to talk about."

"What is this threat Maud? Who is threatening me? Corey sat on the milk crate as Maud gestured to it.

"Not just you dear boy, me as well." Maud took her place on the beanbag. "I feel somewhat responsible too. The men who attacked you last night have put a bounty out on you." Corey's eyes dilated. "Alive of course so that they can teach you a lesson. I need you to listen. They have cut me off from buying for the rest of the month. I will survive but I can't let you come back here."

"Maud I can't leave. I have to finish out this week in Tent City before I can move to another drug." Corey began to wiggle his feet in nervousness. "Honey I have a plan and a goal I have to get back to my family and life soon."

"I know this. Will you just calm down and fucking listen to me, Nancy?" Maud raised her hand causing him to pause and wait in anticipation. "Look do you know where the Chase bank is near Macy's?" Corey nodded. "I need you to meet me there in the morning. I will continue to buy everything you have. What time do you do your next pickup?"

"I pick up at one o'clock every day," Corey said.

"Okay I will give you twenty grand for what you have tonight and I will stash my two safe boxes full over the rest of the week. You can't come back here. Do you understand? I will meet you at two, at the bank, and we will finish up. Now here is the cash." Maud pulled from beside her chair a blue bank bag full of cash. Corey took the bank bag and handed Maud the messenger bag. She then emptied all the

SERUM

blue packs into her lock box and placed the key around the chain on her necklace.

"Now get out of here before they show up. I know they will be early just to find you. Be at the bank at two." Maud turned to Timmy and handed him three packs of meth and said, "Make sure he make it to the cab safely." Timmy nodded and stuck his head out of the tent opening to see if the men from the night before were anywhere to be seen.

Corey followed closely behind Timmy and made it to the tree clearing. Luckily there was a cab dropping off a woman and two small children at the Family Dollar. Corey without saying a word nodded at Timmy and sprinted to the cab.

6

Dr. Miller placed the unidentified man on ice for the night so that dental records and fingerprints could come back. She decided that she would put off the autopsy until she had both results. She may have no ethical sense when it came to her reanimation experiments, but she did when it came to picking the perfect candidate.

CHRISTOPHER MCDONALD

Wednesday started off sluggish for Lacy. She spent the night before running models of her samples through the computer modeling software she found two new variations of the serum that did not break when introduced to the enzymes produced by a corpse. She was sure that this is what made the last experiment so volatile.

She made her usual coffee and decided to take a play from her best friend's playbook. She took the mug over to the wet bar and poured some scotch in the cup. She made it through medical school just fine without becoming an alcoholic but this whole experiment is quickly putting an end to that.

She made her way to the office later than usual hoping in some way that they had found the identity of the man. Unfortunately, no, no name was on her desk. She sat down and looked over her schedule for the day. She had four autopsies to do. It would be a busy day. She decided to do the four and wait.

Autopsy number one was an older woman who died of an apparent heart attack. Lacy did the usual battery of test and found nothing wrong with the woman's heart. The eighty-one-year-old socialite was more than likely poisoned. Lacy sent out for a toxicology screen that should be back by noon.

Autopsy number two was routine. A sixty-one-year-old man died of a stroke. She found a large blood

SERUM

clot in his brain that was the obvious cause of death. Nothing more was suspicious about the autopsy.

While in the middle of the second autopsy the rushed toxicology, report had come back. As suspected the eighty-year-old socialite was poisoned. She had died of a major overdose of blood pressure medications. Not one that she was prescribed either. This was the type of finding that Lacy lived for. She wrote up the death certificate and put cause of death as, homicide by poisoning.

She put a call into the police chief before heading out to lunch. She went to an Irish pub for lunch. Not for the authentic Irish food but for the strong drinks. She needed to block out this anxious feeling about the Joh Doe on ice. She needed to find a way to cope with the stress she was placing on herself over this whole thing.

Returning from lunch after about forty-five minutes, half drunk, she grabbed the file on the third autopsy. Before leaving her office and heading downstairs to start she checked her voicemail to see if there had been a hit on the dental records or prints from her murder victim. Sadly no, she was doomed to wonder longer.

The third autopsy was easy. The man was in hospice for lung cancer. When she opened the chest cavity the lungs were almost unrecognizable. They weighed two pounds too much. The cancer had also begun to spread to the other surrounding organs. Although an easy case, she had a lot of paperwork for this one.

The fourth autopsy was of a man shot in the chest. He was shot by his wife. She admitted it. She was accusing him of cheating. It was an open and shut case. She notated the wounds and such for the prosecution's office, just in case, the defendant come to her senses and lawyered up.

Lacy finished her Wednesday earlier than she thought. It was around four. She went back to her office and checked her voicemail. There were two messages. Both were about her John Doe she was so worried about. The results had come in late on the dental search. There was no match in the database on the dental. The only explanation is that he got the work done overseas or on the black Market. The print search came back from everyone clear with no match.

She left the building with her head held low. She walked to the curb and raised her hand for a cab. One pulled up and she hopped in. "Take me to a hole in the wall bar," she said to the driver.

The driver pulled up outside a bar named the Salty Dog. She looked at the neighborhood and realized this was exactly the distraction she needed. She paid the driver and gave him an extra-large tip for picking such a perfect place.

SERUM

When she walked in there was an older man with grey hair and beard behind the bar puffing on a cigarette. She walked up to the first empty barstool ignoring the stares from the local riffraff.

When she took a seat at the bar the bartender's eyes opened wide. "Well hello pretty lady," he said.

"Hi... I need a stiff one." Lacy sat her three-thousand-dollar purse on the bar next to her.

The bartender chucked as his mind never left the gutter, "What will it be then."

"I will take a greyhound." Lacy said quickly.

"Nice. A salty dog without the salt." The bartender began to mix quickly. He was enamored because women like her never come in to his bar.

He sat the drink down and Lacy began to drink. Hours passed and she ordered one after another. She declined drinks from several men and kept to herself. By six thirty she had had enough. She knew she was way over her limit. She paid the rough bartender and staggered out for a cab.

Right before she made it to the door she felt someone grab her. She turned around and pushed the man. The bar fell silent. She pulled from her side purse pocket her ME badge. It looked like an NYPD badge.

"Back off fucker," she said. The man raised his hands in response and let her walk out.

Once in the cab she knew she had to go home but her OCD would not let her. She gave the driver the address of her office. She made it there a little after seven and the place was dark. She swiped her badge and went inside.

She sat in her office and pondered for a while. She wanted Mark to come by so bad but did not dare call him. She took off her hills and placed them under her desk. She swapped them for a pair of tennis shoes she kept in her closet.

After a while she got to her feet and made it to the basement. She walked to the lab and grabbed her coat. She stuffed the gloves in her pocket and began to prepare the syringes with one of the two she thought would work. Serum 105 is the one she went with. As she filled the heavy-duty metal syringe with the glowing blue liquid; she felt the anxiety rush over her.

She was alone and if something happened she was done. 'Please let this work,' she said to herself.

She walked to the Morgue and wheeled a gurney to the cooler doors. She pulled the drawer out and exposed the bag. She had no problems placing the gurney next to the drawer and sliding the body bag over. The bag cracked as she did so.

"Here we go John. Let's see what you have told us." She wheeled the gurney over to the autopsy

SERUM

table and did another transfer with more crackling from the bag. After she maneuvered him onto the table she worked him out of the bag starting with the feet.

She paused to look at the man. "I hope to hell this works." She went ahead and prepared the dose of potassium and began to prep herself.

Like before Lacy leaned the head forward and injected the first amount of glowing liquid at the base of his brain stem. She then stepped back and waited. She wanted to give it a few minutes. If this serum worked better than the other one she may not need as much.

After the five minutes passed she moved to the eyes. As before she carefully placed the needle behind each of the eyeballs. She waited another five minutes. Nothing was happening.

Thinking that this trial would also end badly she opened the mouth to inject the last bit into the soft pallet. As she opened the mouth she notice a bright color glowing from inside the mouth. The serum was in the veins inside the mouth. "Fuck... It's working."

She stepped back and sat the remainder of the serum back on a tray. She watched as the veins in his temple had a glowing light pulse through them and back into the brain. It was working. This both frightened Lacy and excited her.

She watched as the eyelids of the corpse began to quiver. The lips followed and began to quiver. The jaw clamped down and Lacy could hear the teeth begin to grind. She had a rush of adrenalin and picked up the potassium syringe.

All at once the corpses face went calm and relaxed. They eyes slowly opened and she heard a noise. It took some time for her to realize what the noise was. The corpse was moaning.

Lacy observed for a few moments before walking over to the body. When she had the courage, she walked over. When she made it to the side of the body the eyes turned and stared at her. The head remained facing upward but the eyes began to go crazy. They went from looking at her to the celling to the other side of the room.

The eyes found her again and fixed their gaze at her. "Help me" The corpse said with a whisper.

"I'm Dr. Miller. What's your name?" Dr. Miller walked over and stood over the head of the corpse.

"I'm Charlie. I can't move! My voice isn't loud." The corpse sounded panicked.

Dr. Miller paused and thought for a moment. She had no idea what to say. She had no idea what to do at this point. "Charlie... I need you to stay calm. I will explain everything in due time. I need you to tell me your last name."

SERUM

The corpse blinked and said in a faint weak voice. "Townsend.. I'm Charlie Townsend."

"Good..." Dr. Miller replied. "Now what is the last thing you remember?"

Again, the corpse began to blink. "I was shot... He was mugging me. He shot me... Am I paralyzed?"

"I will get to that soon. Now what did the man look like?" Dr. Miller leaned in as the corpse began to blink again.

After a moment of silence. Charlie began to have facial convulsions. Dr. Miller felt the neck for a pulse out of reflex. The man was dead so of course there was none to feel. The face faded and relaxed.

Dr. Miller waited thirty minutes before, and as a safety measure injected the potassium behind the eyeball. She did her job and completed the autopsy. She released the death certificate to the police after fudging some things in her report to reflect how she knew the identity.

7

On Friday, as usual Lacy and Mark met at a nice restaurant for lunch. They both sat and ordered cocktails.

152

"I see you are on board with this whole alcoholism thing." Mark said as he looked over the menu.

"It worked Mark..." Lacy said in a whispering voice.

Never taking his eyes off the menu he said. "What worked?"

"The serum worked. I found the identity of a body in my morgue." Lacy said as the waiter sat down the scotch on the table.

Mark dropped both his jaw and his menu. "Are you fucking kidding, Lacy... You did it again.. "

"Yes, Mark and it worked. He was ab e to tell me his name." Lacy took a large gulp of scotch. Mark turned in disapproval looking at the TV over the bar as Anderson Cooper reported on the Middle East.

"I can't believe you. You promised me you would not do this again. You know what will happen if they figure something out. I can't save you... You will go to jail." Mark downed his entire drink waving for the bartender to bring another round.

"I know Mark but I had to. I had to find out. I told the police I found dental records. He went out on me before I could get a description of the killer. The family will know what happened to him now " Lacy sat back in her chair. The bartender sat down a drink in front of each of them.

"Enough about that. How is Corey? Has he been writing?" Lacy took a sip.

SERUM

Fuming in anger he said, "he is fine. He thinks he has a week left and he can come home." Mark went back to not looking at her and looking at the TV to show his disapproval.

"That's great!" She said finishing off the second drink. "I really missed..." She was interrupted by Mark placing his hands on hers not taking his eyes off the TV.

She turned to look as CNN was reporting of a body missing from a New York City funeral home. The crawl read "The body of Charlie Townsend is believed to have been stolen from an NYC funeral home early this morning."

Mark took his eyes off the TV and looked at Lacy. "What was his name?"

CHAPTER 8

SERUM

Corey woke up Monday ready to start the week. He had plenty of rest and was ready to start the job he originally went undercover for. He had sacrificed so much and this day is what it all had boiled down to. He hopped he could make this his last five days and be home by the weekend.

Thanks to Maud, Corey had made himself a small fortune. He had amassed over fifty thousand in cash and was ready to hit the heroin Market hard and finish by Friday.

Corey went ahead and got his usual shower and prepared to strap the camera system to his body. He was lucky that it was cool enough to have a jacket this week. He had to conceal the battery pack of the recording equipment.

He thought to himself as he finished getting dressed. 'Everyone can see that this is not me. Everyone keeps telling me to get out as soon as I can. With any luck, I will."

Corey grabbed his bag of cash and headed out the door locking, it up behind him. Leaving only his clothes in the apartment now. He walked down the stairs. As he made it to the lobby he ran into his landlord Mr. Bill.

"Hey kid how, the hell are you." Bill said while putting the key in the office door. "Did you have a good weekend buddy?"

Corey walked over to him as he was struggling with the lock and said. "Yes, sir I rested most of the weekend. I hope to be moving on soon. I promise to bring the key by and clean the place for you before I go."

Bill dropped his ring of keys in the floor. "You are going to do what?" Bill bent over to pick up the keys. He couldn't decide if he had done it due to shock or nervousness that he might be losing the one good tenant he ever had. "Never mind buddy. You do what's best for you. I can tell you don't belong here. You need to move on if you are ready."

"Thank you, Mr. Bill. This has been a great place to stay." Corey followed him into the office and watched as he started messing with his coffee pot.

"Don't worry about the cleaning. I pay some crack head thirty bucks a unit to come by and clean for me. You just get the hell up out of here and move to greener pastures." Bill finished up setting the coffee pot on and pressed the red 'on' button.

"I will Mr. Bill. You have a great Monday." Corey nodded and hopped out of the office with a bit of a spring in his step. He knew that when all was said and done he would have some great stories to tell his new child.

Corey went on down the street and made it to the corner Starbucks as usual. It was the start of the pumpkin spice craze. So of course, he had to get in on it. He loved the pumpkin spice flavored latte.

SERUM

Corey walked down the street and decided to head over to the Salty Dog. He needed to celebrate. He also needed to kill some time before going to his pickup. Here it was just ten in the morning and he was going to be drinking at the bar. He would probably even eat some crummy bar food.

When he made it to the Salty Dog he read a sign outside the door:

Adult Daycare Rules

No Outside Food or Drinks, No Pets. (Unless a Spouse)

Shoes and Shirt Required or No Service

Corey finished up the pumpkin spice latte outside the door and threw the empty cup in the container next to the door. When he walked in he was amazed at the number of people in there this time of the morning. Corey almost didn't have a spot at the bar.

Corey sat next to a rather well-dressed man and a woman in scrubs. While waiting on the rough Brooklyn bartender he listened in on their conversation. The pair had obviously just got off work at the local hospital. The well-dressed man was a doctor of sorts in the ER and the nurse and he were close to say the least.

"Hey there welcome back. What would you like to drink?" The man with the grey beard said as he slapped his hand on the counter in front of Corey

Learning from his mistake a couple days ago he said' "I will take a bud light draft." The bartender saying nothing opened up the cooler retrieving a frosted mug. After filling it he sat the beer in front of Corey. "What time does your kitchen open?'

"Buddy we are open twenty-four seven, three sixty-five. We will serve you on Christmas day at six am if you like." The bartender leaned against the bar like he had been rehearsing that spiel for years.

"Oh great!" Corey said. "I'll take a cheese burger and fries."

"Coming right up." The bartender said. He was in a better mood today. Corey thought he must not be a night person.

"Wow this truly is 'The City that Never Sleeps.'" Corey said out loud to himself.

"You are right about that one." The well-dressed man sitting next to him said. "This is one of the best places to come grab a drink and some good food."

"I found this place last week. Now I know that it's here if I ever need it." Corey took out his burner phone to look at the time. Of course, he had plenty of time.

"Well I work in the ER at the hospital down the road. I get off at eight in the morning. Sometimes

159

SERUM

later depending. This is the closest place for me to get some decent food that's not breakfast and a drink before I get some sleep." He picked up his cocktail in a cheers gesture.

"Yeah I moved to this part of town for work and needed a place to unwind before a stressful shift." Corey also picked up his beer in a cheers gesture. "I'm Corey, by the way."

"Bob... Bob Shaw." The man and Corey took a sip of their beverage in unison.

About the time Corey had finished up his first drink the grumpy older man was setting a plate with his burger and fries in front of him. "I will take a scotch and soda this time." Catching himself before the bartender could ask his condescending question Corey said, "Well scotch is fine."

"Right away buddy." The man sat his cigarette in the ash tray in front of Corey and started making his drink. The smoke billowed from the ashtray straight to Corey's nose. The smell maze him sneeze. "Gazuntite" the bartender said as he sat the drink in front of him.

Corey began to eat listening to the conversation between the doctor and the nurse. As he ate he got a great ear full about the politics of a hospital. Corey thought that the drug trade was bad. The doctor was explaining to the nurse that they were enacting a biometric security update using fingerprints due to the recent security breach. The nurse asked if he ever found his ID badge.

Corey finished the burger and picked at the fries. The bartender returned as he pushed the basket to the edge of the bar signaling he was done. "Want another scotch or beer?" The barkeep asked.

"Yeah keep them coming I need a little liquid courage before I deal with what I have to deal with." Corey patted the counter as he spoke.

"Boy sounds serious," the bartender said as he scooped up the glass of the bar top.

Shortly after he returned with a fresh scotch drink the doctor said, "There is nothing better than a stiff scotch to give you courage."

Corey lifted the fresh drink and said, 'Cheers to that!" The doctor reciprocated and lifted his bottled Corona to clink with Corey.

Corey continued to drink through the morning ordering one after another. By the time it was time to leave for the pickup he had a forty-dollar tab and had consumed five scotches, two beers, and a hamburger basket. Considering the amount, he consumed it was great the tab was as small as it was.

Corey handed the bartender three twenties and told him to keep the change. The bartender thanked him graciously as he tried to stand. It was difficult but he managed.

The doctor asked, "You're not driving are you buddy?"

SERUM

Corey replied, "Never..." To that he began walking to the door of the crummy little hole in the wall named The Salty Dog.

Once on the street Corey realized quickly how drunk he actually was. Instead of getting a cab he decided it would do him some good to walk off some of the booze. This was the most drunk Corey ever was trying to walk down the sidewalks of New York. He would have to stop from time to time so that he could catch his balance leaning against a mail drop or a lamp post.

One lamp post he came to, he noticed birds, eating some fries where someone tried to throw them in a trash can but Missed. With it being fall the birds were happy and fat. He continued on his way to the apartment building stumbling and looking back like there was something that had actually tripped him. Of course, there was nothing. He was just drunk off his ass.

He made it to the building a little early. Corey decided to prop himself against a lamp post outside the building for the fifteen minutes before his pickup time. He didn't want to do anything to aggravate Pedro and his girls. As he stood there he watched the people on the street. One in particular caught his eye. A black male about six-five walking toward the building with an empty duffle bag. Corey knew instantly that this was the pickup before his

Corey walked up the stairs with a minute to spare. He passed the black man coming down. He heard the rattling of the plastic baggies in the now full duffle bag. The two exchanged glances and knew without saying a word what the other was there for. Corey paused for a second outside the door trying to gather his strength to argue.

Corey snapped his fingers and opened the door. He was greeted by Pedro. "Joto... How are you? Hope you had a good weekend."

"I'm good Pedro. My weekend was fine I stayed drunk the entire time." Corey said while placing the messenger bag on the counter.

Pedro passed the bag to one of the women in black dress and stilettos. "Are you ready for this Joto. You wanted to join the big boys this week right?"

Corey watched as Pedro walked to fridge and pulled two Coors Lights from inside. "Yes, I want to join the big dogs. I'm ready. I have the cash needed and I think I have learned the trade."

Pedro tossed the Coors Light over to Corey. Luckily in his drunk state he was able to catch it. "Well Looking from the wad of cash you have just enough to get started. We will give you plenty to start off with."

"So, you're not going to fight me on it like you have been for weeks?" Corey asked.

SERUM

"Joto get it straight. You came to us with only a small stack of hundreds. You had to build up to this. We will be selling you the Heroin for ninety a pack. You need to be ready for this." Pedro popped the top on his beer and took a sip.

"Ready for what?" Corey asked.

"You are in the big league now Joto. There will be competition for the dollar. When you get to the park tonight you will not be the only dealer there. You will have a slight advantage being new. The high-end buyers will know you are not smart enough to cut the shit before selling it." Pedro took a post-it note from one of his women counting the cash.

Pedro nodded at the other woman to begin packing the bag handing the post-it over to her for processing. "Listen Joto, listen carefully. There will be others in the park. You have to go in knowing what you are doing. The night you meet me you saw I was next to one of the public restrooms. This is where you need to start. This is where you will do a lot of one or two bag purchases from the bums."

Corey popped the top on his beer realizing he was sobering up too quickly. "I have to deal with more bums. I thought this was a higher end product?"

"Are you goanna let me finish?" Corey nodded. "Ok then, the bums will more than likely stay in the park after you leave to turn a profit on it. That's ok.

They just clean up the mess for you. They are the real one risking getting caught when they start to close the park, and officers begin the sweep. You will be long gone by then.

When you get to an unoccupied restroom you will need to stake out next to the men's entrance. That's where people walking the patch will be looking. You stand and people will walk up and ask how much. I would say to stay firm with two-hundred. Only drop if the bum only has one-eighty or so."

Pedro paused to take another drink. Corey had a large gulp as well taking what he was saying in. "When you have finished it should be good and dark. You will then move your steak out to a park bench."

Pedro took a piece of white chalk from his drawer in the money counting table. "You will use this chalk to Mark that you are open for business. This will be for the high-end clients that will be bringing larger quantities of cash to you. They pretend to be runners and will sit on the bench next to you when they notice the chalk."

"Where do I Mark that I'm open at?" Corey asked.

"Ok yeah. You will need to find a bench close to a water fountain. Take the chalk and make a ring on the base. That way the joggers know when you are selling. One of the homeless crew will use your bench after you leave to clean up."

SERUM

Pedro downed the rest of the can and threw it away in the trash can next to the door, shooting it like a basketball. "I need to warn you Joto you will see some prominent figures in the park. You will be up town. Do not get all-star struck. They won't buy from you. Treat them like any other buyer."

Pedro handed Corey the bag and piece of chalk. "Do you have anything else you want to ask?"

Corey took the bag and the piece of chalk. "I think I have it. As long as I can make it out before the cops close the place I will be fine."

With that Pedro nodded and motioned to the door. Corey walked out and down the stairs. He felt his buzz almost completely faded. It was the stress or the fifteen minutes. He didn't quite know which. He decided he would head over to the nicer part of town and sit at a bar there until dusk.

2

Dr. Miller was called early this particular Monday. She was awoken by Detective Cox. Apparently there was a murder on the edge of the city that looked fishy to him. She got her stuff together, walking out the door, forgetting to brush her teeth.

She thought of a Kesha song from when she was in school, "Before I leave brush my teeth with a bottle of Jack."

Because of the distance and the fact, it was work related she decided to take UBER using the city expense card. The driver was prompt as promised, five minutes. She hopped in and rode to the edge of the city where the crime occurred. She was shocked that they even called her. The crime was nearly outside of her jurisdiction.

When she pulled into the strip shopping center, the entire front of the Family Dollar had been taped off with yellow caution tape. There on the pavement were two bodies. There were several police and several onlookers. She stepped out of the black town car observing the crowd. They all looked out of place and worn down.

As she approached the tape she pulled her ME badge from her purse along with some gloves. She passed by an ambulance and meet Will at the tape line. "Will, what do we have this early Monday morning?"

"Well it looks a little funny. All these people here act like they know the victims but none say they saw what happened." Detective Cox spoke while holding the tape up for Dr. Miller. "They are over here in front of the store entrance."

Dr. Miller walked to the front of the store. Next to the door were two coin operated children's

SERUM

riding toys. One a spaceship, the other was a race car. The victims were sitting in the ridding toys. The woman was place in the rocket ship and the man was placed in the race car.

"Wow they were killed then propped up here?' Lacy asked the detective.

"Looks that way Miss. The blood is all out in the center of the parking lot." He pointed to the area Marked with evidence Markers. "It looks like they were placed here. One thing that's strange is the old woman was alive when the ambulance got here but not long. She said two words to the EMT before she bled out."

"Wow. This is gory." Lacy put the gloves on and pulled the covers for her shoes out of her purse. "Have your guys stand back Will and let me do my thing."

"Will do Doc." The detective waved his arms letting the others know to give the ME the crime scene.

Dr. Miller started to the center of the parking lot where she began to examine the blood. It was pooled in two distinct puddles. Without ever seeing the bodies she knew by the pattern that it was a knife killing. They were bled then propped up in the riding toys. One puddle had a line leading to the entrance. "They were dragged by two or more people." She spoke out loud so that Detective Cox could hear standing ten feet away.

She then followed the trail of blood to the front of the Family Dollar. She looked first at the male. Propped up in the race car his head rested against the wall. His eyes were open and ante mortem brushing on his right cheek and jaw. "He was beaten before killed." She then examined the laceration along the neck. The cut was sloppy and jagged. "The blade was dull. He sawed at his neck for a couple minutes. We will probably find some flesh in the pools of blood over there." Again, she spoke so the detective could take note.

She walked to the spaceship. She noticed the condition of the toy. The tip was broken. The thought how some kid wouldn't care. In their mind, they would still be traveling to Mars.

The woman sat back. Her neck wasn't cut. She moved in closer and noticed what had killed her. The perp had slit her wrist laterally from the palm to the elbow. "She bled out slow. That's why the EMT found her alive still. "

Lacy had seen all she needed to before the bodies were bagged. She walked over to William. "What are their names?"

"Have no clue. None of the people weeping over there are willing to say. If they ever really knew." William pointed to the people standing next to the tape line crying and looking for answers.

SERUM

Dr. Miller walked to the tape line and began to stare down the crowd. She paced on the other side of the tape. "If anyone knows who these two people are please speak up. They need justice." She continued to pace like a cat in a cage. No one spoke up. All she heard was weeping.

Will walked up behind her and said, "We have been trying all morning. No one will speak. Whoever did this probably threatened all of them too. We will have to rely on good ole detective work and science."

Lacy looked at him shaking her head. "Will do, you even have a clue as to why?"

"Not a single clue." Detective cox said.

Dr. Miller started to walk to the assistant medical examiner waiting on her order to move the body. She stopped at the blood puddle with Will still behind her. "What did she say?"

"What did who say?" William asked.

"The old woman. What did she say to the EMT?" Lacy turned to face Detective Cox.

"Oh... 'Protect Corey.'" Detective Cox noticed a change in Dr. Miller's expression. "We can only guess that's the name of the guy. That's all we have to go on.

Lacy turned and began a brisk walk to the tape line motioning to the assistant ME to begin.

3

Corey found himself sitting at a nice outdoor cafe of what use to the Palace Hotel. He ordered mimosas to start with then found a particular vintage of wine he and Mark enjoyed. Opus One 1999 was on sale for a mere six hundred a bottle. He ordered the bottle.

The waiter came over every fifteen minutes or so to refill the glass. As dusk began to approach Corey paid his tab and downed the last bit of the Opus One ending his all-day-drunk.

Corey stumbled across the sidewalk and headed to the park entrance across from the hotel. Dusk had not quite fallen so it gave him some time to find a spot to set up shop. He began to walk the park following the signs to the restroom. He comes upon the first one facing the grand walk. There was the black male he had seen coming from the pickup apartment. The man noticed Corey right away and shook his head no.

Corey moved on. He noticed that there were a fair number of park benches and water fountains to chalk up for business. He was amazed the number of people in the park this late in the evening. He walked turning down side paths. Finally, he found one path with a restroom not really facing anything that needed someone to set up shop.

SERUM

Corey stood there looking at the ground as he heard a click that startled him. Then came a low humming noise. He looked from side to side to find the source. Nothing in sight. He then noticed it was the sodium outdoor light on the restroom clicking on. It was getting dark so they helped light the paths. Shortly after the outdoor lights on the building lit the lamp post began to light one by one lighting even more of the park.

All around him he could see the bright lights of the city coming through the trees. Corey looked from side to side to see if someone was coming to buy. He saw no one. He looked at the ground and thought he must be in the right place. Someone had been standing here for a while recently. There were cigarette butts on the ground in almost a circle around where he stood.

Corey looked up from the cigarettes to see someone coming down the path. The person looked to be Hispanic. He was a tall thin man and had a bag over his shoulder much like Corey's. The man was smoking on a cigarette as he approached. He looked up and glanced at Corey. The Hispanic man paused and threw his cigarette to the ground.

Corey realized he was in the man's spot. Corey felt a rush of adrenalin and fear comes over him. He didn't know if he needed to reach for his gun or just stand there. After a couple of seconds, what seemed like hours, the man turned and headed back the way he came.

Corey, not realizing he had been holding his breath, let all the air in his lungs out with a whoosh. He felt the nervous perspiration run down his back. This reminded him to reach to his back and flip on the camera system he had attached earlier. He would have been pissed if he had come all this way and actually sold drugs to the actor without having his camera on to catch the transaction.

Shortly after he flipped the power on the recorder Corey noticed a group of people approaching. He hopped this was not yet another turf confrontation. Looking at the five-people approaching him quickly sized up the fact these were his clients. One leading the group looked twelve.

As the posse approached the young leader spoke. "You are new. Where is Jose?"

To this Corey replied, "He is somewhere else in the park." He realized they were talking about the cigarette smoking Latino from a couple minutes ago.

"How much a pack?" The small but confident leader spoke.

"How old are you?" Corey asked.

"Do you want to make a sale or not?" The boy said. "This is drugs not lottery tickets or cigarettes. Now how fucking much?"

SERUM

Corey shocked to hear the young boy speak like that. "Two-hundred," he said.

The boy turned to the others. Corey noticed they were people like the ones that lived in Tent City, homeless looking. "What did you cut it with?" The boy asked looking back at Corey.

"I don't cut my stash. I sell it like I pick it up." Corey watched the boy's face never wavering.

"Sure, man that's what they all say." The boy turned back to the group and waited for approval. Between the four behind the boy they come up with six-hundred dollars. The boy straitened the cash and handed it over to Corey. Corey in return counted and stuffed it in the back pouch of his bag next to the firearm Maud gave him. In return, he grabbed three packs and handed them to the boy. Saying nothing they group turned and walked off.

While Corey watched the group leave he wondered about the boy and his friends. Where did they come from? Where were they going? Were the drugs for them?

Corey's thought was broken when he heard a snap of a branch as someone approached from the tee line. Corey spun around to see who was coming. Every noise seemed to startle him. He looked to see another two-people approaching. This time not from a path but the center of the park.

CHRISTOPHER MCDONALD

This time the transaction went much faster. The two asked how much. Corey told them and then they purchased then moved on. One after the other groups and single people come. Some had hundred dollar bills and some had spare change basically. Everyone bought that approached him. After about an hour he decided the traffic was dead at the restroom. He decided to move on to the bench.

He walked out from the public restroom area to a surprise. There were tens of people running along the track. He found a bench not too far from the restroom that had a water fountain next to it. Corey pulled the chalk from his pack and marked the unmarked water fountain. He wondered how many times this one fountain had been Marked over the years. He sat in the park bench waiting for his next customer. He waited with one after the other passing him by. He wondered if they had their usua person and that's why. Was he too early to the bench?

About to give up hope someone stopped to tie their shoe, that did not need tied, in front of him. The woman turned to look at him to say, "Are you open?"

He looked from side to side before he realized she was talking to him. "Yeah I'm open. Sit here", as he patted the seat next to him. Corey said, before she could ask, "its two a pack." Corey noticed the woman looked very familiar. She handed him four, one - hundred dollar bills. Corey took two packs from his

SERUM

bag and she stuffed them in her outfit and jumped up to restart her jog.

After she ran off Corey realized where he knew her from. She was a co-host on one of those morning shows filmed up the street near Time Square. She was the one that only republicans can stand. Boy if people knew. He had footage of her. He thought if he didn't get the man he was hired to, he would at least have the tape of a controversial celebrity.

He sat watching the people walking and running. One after the other he had customers that shocked and awed him. There was even a couple walking their dog, a Great Dane, who bought from him. The woman, he noticed, was wearing Prada.

He sold out quickly and decided to walk around the park. He was curious as to the diverse clientèle. He could not imagine he and Mark walking their dog (if they had one) and picking up five packs of heroin. He was able to spot his competition while walking. He actually noticed one man. He was the man that walked down the path at the restroom. Corey just nodded and walked past him. He acknowledged the gesture and went on waiting on his next client.

Corey made it half way around the gigantic park when he noticed yet another dealer. He recognized him quickly and dodged behind a tree. He hoped the man didn't see him. His stomach began to ache. Corey didn't know if it was because the dealer had kicked the shit out of him, or if it were nerves.

As Corey looked around from the tree he noticed two other of the man's posse hanging out around the nearby restroom. Corey decided he would head back the way he came as quickly as possible trying not to attract attention. As he began to walk briskly back the way he came one of the men at the restroom became curious and started to follow Corey.

Corey felt the man's eyes trained on the back of his head. This made his heart rush. He picked up the pace. And darted to the trail leading to the exit sign. Once out of the park Corey turned to see the man who followed. The man's eyes widened as he realized who Corey was and how they all knew one another. Corey turned and ran opening the flap of his briefcase and put his hand on the gun Maud gave him. The man never left the park but Corey knew his presence was known.

4

Lacy had the cab stop off at Starbucks about a block from the morgue. While in line waiting on her drink she decided to text Mark and see if he had heard from Corey and if he was alright. Mark sent a text back as she picked up her cup of espresso and

SERUM

steamed milk. He had heard from Corey, and hopping this was the last week he had to be under cover.

She sighed with relief as she walked out of the busy coffee shop. She knew it was a million in one chance that Corey was the Corey the old woman referred to. She decided to walk the rest of the way back to the office and do some research on the Missing body before the two new corpses arrived.

She walked into the lobby of her building and the receptionist stood to greet her. "Dr. Miller," the young blonde woman said. "You have someone from the FBI in your office."

Lacy's eyes dilated and she suddenly became nervous. "The FBI? Wonder why? Thank you." Lacy walked down to her office. When she walked in the door there was a tall man in a black suit sitting in a chair across from her desk.

The agent stood to great her. He took out his credential wallet He flipped it open and said. "Special Agent Ratcliff, Miss. I am here to ask you a few questions about the body missing from the Harrison Brothers Funeral Home."

Lacy motioned for him to sit. "That is the first thing I was going to do this morning. I wanted to know if he was one of ours. The name sounds familiar. Of course, it could be a coincidence seeing how it is the same name from Charlie's Angels." Lacy took her seat and the agent sat as well.

"The funeral home tells us the body came from your Morgue. I wanted to know if I could see the autopsy report on Mister Townsend."

"I can give you what we have but the file will be incomplete until results of blood work and everything else comes back. I can't rule a cause of death until then." Lacy spoke while turning on her computer. "I will just look up his file."

The agent put his badge back in his inner coat pocket. After a few minutes of silence her computer finally was ready for her to look up the fine. The whole time her heart was in her shoes. She hoped that the nervousness didn't show. She looked at the screen for a couple of minutes before speaking.

To her surprise the test results were back. "It looks like the results are back and were entered this morning. Ahhh it also looks like I did the autopsy toc." She took her eyes off the computer and looked at him. "Give me a few seconds and I will go fetch the file and write up the COD for you."

He nodded his head and Lacy walked out of the office. While she was out of the room the detective stood and began looking around the room. He looked at all of her pictures on the desk and the diplomas and medals on the wall. After about ten minutes she returned with a blue file. She said as she handed it over to the agent, "All ready. I just need for you to sign the chain of custody form here and you can be on your way."

Lacy flipped open the file and pointed at the spots for him to fill out. The agent took his time reading the form and finally filled out everything and handed it over. The agent looked at her and said, "I will be in touch if I have any questions. Also, this goes without saying if the body ends up back here I need you to give me a call." He pulled out a card from a card holder from his trouser pocket.

"Will do," Lacy said.

"I can see myself out. Thank you doctor." Agent Ratcliff walked toward the door. He paused and looked back at her making her even more nervous. "You are a very accomplished woman."

This almost made her blush and probably would have if she was not so nervous about the whole thing. "Thank you sir," she replied. The agent then walked on out the door. She went to her chair and sunk in it like a rock sinking into water. She was scared.

She thought of all of the possibilities. She hoped that the one that actually happened was someone stole the body. She was scared to death at the other thought. It was just as plausible as the other option. She instantly rejected the thought.

'The serum was designed for the head only,' she thought. 'The notion that it caused the body to walk out of there is absolutely preposterous.' She picked up the cup of coffee and took a sip. By this time the coffee was completely cold.

The phone rang breaking her train of thought. It was the morgue office letting her know the two bodies were here from the crime scene earlier. She took her cold coffee with her as she headed to the elevator.

Once downstairs she put her coffee n the microwave. After it was heated she went to the main room. There before her were two bodies fresh out of the bags. The young boys were stained in blood. The blood on the clothes and skin was starting to turn brown.

She walked to the boy and looked him over. The neck wound was so deep it cut through his vocal cords. She caught herself mid thought. She realized what it was she was doing. She was sizing him up for a serum trial. She knew instantly he was no candidate because of the fact he wouldn't be able to tell her anything. 'He could blink yes or no to her answers.' She thought.

She turned and focused her attention on the old woman. The woman who warned of Corey. "You... You could tell me something." She spoke aloud to the corpse. She walked around the body. Looking it up and down for a clue. She turned the hands over and

SERUM

examined the wound. It was more than likely done by the same blade. She noted to herself that because of the woman's age and poor health she had terribly thin skin.

Lacy left the room and told her other MEs that she would do the autopsy herself on the woman later today and they could start the prep on them both. She assigned the boy to another ME in the building to be done that day.

Lacy retired to her private lab where she would prep for the autopsy. She knew without second-guessing that she would use the serum on the old woman. Her curiosity and passion for the truth overwhelmed her. She needed to know if the Corey she spoke of was her Corey. Well, Mark and her Corey.

She pulled up her computer and opened a molecular testing application. She decided to run scenarios on the last serum she tested on the Missing Charlie from a local funeral home. She tested the compound on everything she could think of. She looked at the different chemicals formed during the decomposition process. She also pulled all the different chemicals found in the embalming fluids put in bodies. She found nothing.

After hours and hours of research she surfaced the lab to head to lunch. She text Mark and told him to meet her at the Four Seasons bar for lunch, that she needed a drink. He replied quickly and said he was on his way.

Before leaving the building she looked in to see if the boy had an ID or the body turned up anything interesting. Sadly, no print or dental match. The ME told Dr. Miller that he had never had any dental work. She did however find signs of meth use while examining the oral cavity.

Dr. Miller hopped a cab directly outside her building for the trip down town. When she made it to the Four Seasons she paused to look at the park across the street. She marveled at how peaceful and tranquil it looked. People running in mid-day. Old people walking their dogs and mom's letting their kids have playdates with other kids. She didn't notice but she stared at the park for a good five minutes until she felt a tap on her shoulder.

"You ok Lacy? You look like you have seen a ghost?" Mark said watching her startled reaction to him.

"I'm fine... We have to talk." She motioned to him and walked to the front door of the hotel.

Once inside she led him straight to the bar. This time of day there was only one other person at the bar. A business man in a five-thousand-dollar suit. They sat directly in the center of the bar and Lacy waived the barkeep over.

SERUM

"We will take two eighteen-year-old scotches on the rocks please." Lacy ordered not waiting if this was something Mark even wanted this early. She just knew. He was worried and would be even more worried after she got done with the conversation.

"I need to tell you something, Mark, and I hope it's nothing. I have a dead woman in the morgue. She was alive when the EMT got there this morning. She looks like she was tortured or something for information." Mark looked at Lacy saying nothing just sipping on the drink the bartender brought. "She was in a rough part of town. She said something to the EMT that I just can't get out of my mind."

Mark watched as she picked up her glass to take a drink. "Well go on..." He said while watching her down the entire glass of scotch and motion for another.

"She told the EMT to, 'Protect Corey.' Now... That's why I text you earlier. Do we have no way of getting in in touch with him?" Lacy didn't wait on him to answer. "Now I am going to tell you I am going to use the serum again to wake her up. I can't on the boy that was found with her. I can however on her."

Mark downed his entire drink with one gulp too. Motioned for the barkeep to bring him another as well. "Lacy you can't use that again. You don't even know yet if that's the reason the body went missing."

"That's another thing I need to tell you. I may need an attorney. I had a visit from an FBI agent this morning. He wanted the file on Mr. Townsend. I of course gave it to him without haste and he said he would be in touch." Lacy grabbed the new scotch drink and this time took a small sip as she was feeling warm already from the first glass.

Mark slumped down on the bar and leaned his head over his new glass of scotch. "Lacy what have we gotten ourselves in to?"

Lacy just looked at him for a second. "We... Nothing... You were never part of it and never knew. I am now elbows deep. Maybe not but if so I need you. I also need to know if it is our Corey."

Mark looked up and tried to interrupt her. She wouldn't let him and continued. "I know... Before you say anything listen to the facts. This woman may be talking about another Corey indeed. If not, I need to know. You need to know so we can find him and get him out."

Mark nodded his head and said, "What facts?"

"Fact number one. The boy that was found with the old woman was using meth. I looked in on his autopsy before coming here. Fact number two. The two were found in a known drug neighborhood. There are many deaths reported here." She drank some more scotch looking at Mark.

SERUM

"Lacy there has to be hundred guys in the city, slinging drugs, named Corey." Mark looked back down at his scotch.

"Don't you want to know? Don't you need to know?" She asked.

Mark just looked up at her and killed this glass of scotch. She spoke up, "I am going to use the serum on her today at four. I can do it alone. I have the hang of it by now at least."

Mark just stared blankly at her until the barkeep asked if he wanted another scotch. He nodded his head yes and said to Lacy. "Do it..."

Looking surprised at what he said she replied. "Thanks Mark but I wasn't looking for permission. I was informing you. I am going to do this and we are going to go get Corey's ass if it turns out to be him. Four-hundred-thousand or not."

Mark just nodded his head in agreement. "We may never live this down if we pull him off this and he is this close to the finish line."

"Mark, that's the least of my worries right now don't you think. There is a body out there with my compound in it. Who knows how this is going to end." Lacy looked up the barkeep and said, "Keep them coming." Then she downed what was left of her third drink.

After a healthy lunch of alcohol, she took a cab back to the morgue. She could feel her gut rumbling from no food and all the booze. After she got back to the building she headed straight back to her lab. She was determined to test the next sample on the computer for anomalies.

She ran every scenario she could think of on the computer modeling program. After she noticed it was a little after four and the bottom floor would be cleared of all personnel soon, she put on her lab coat. As she reached for the cooler containing the Serum there was a knock at the door.

It was the ME doing the autopsy on the boy. He said, "I thought you would want to know we never found an ID on the boy. He was probably a runaway or something."

"Thank you..." Dr. Miller said and nodded to him. He headed to the elevator.

Dr. Miller shut the door and went back to the case and opened the door. This serum she pulled from within was glowing like the rest. This time the radioactive glow was green. She thought of a Simpson's episode where Homer's nuclear plant exploded and left behind green goo.

She filled the syringe with the glowing green solution. She sat it on a tray and opened the door. Before leaving she poked her head out making sure everyone had gone for the day. They had so she walked the short distance to the main body room.

SERUM

When she got in the large autopsy room the body of the old woman was completely stripped and cleaned with a white sheet over her, fresh from processing. Dr. Miller sat the tray with the serum on the table next to where the body lay. She took a deep breath and uncovered the head and upper chest.

Looking at the woman she paused to think. 'What will you ask her if she is only awake for a second? You have to be quick. You don't want to waste time with meaningless chit chat if she is going to be out as soon as she is reanimated. Lacy took another deep breath and picked up the syringe.

The green glow danced across the woman's wrinkled skin as she lifted the head up. She felt for the spot-on neck where she needed to put the needle in. While propping up the head with one hand she used her right hand to plunge the needle in. The injection site made a squishing and cracking noise as the glowing fluid went in.

Lacy let the head down to rest on the autopsy table again. As she moved from one side of the table to the next, so she could get a better grip for the next injection, she noticed something strange. Well she noticed something strange under the circumstances. The green liquid was moving through the veins in the temple region.

CHRISTOPHER MCDONALD

Dr. Miller stood and watched as the green faded and moved into the head. She decided to holc off on the next injection and wait to see of the serum would migrate and populate on its own. She stood back away from the body and watched. She wanted to see a reaction. If she did that would mean this was the one.

After about fifteen minutes with no reaction what-so-ever she moved on to the eye sockets. She lifted the right upper eye lid to reveal the most beautiful blue eyes she had ever seen. She moved the eye down and placed the needle in the tissue behind the eye. She gave a slight push of the plunger and injected some serum. She did the same behind the left eye.

As she was pulling the needle out of the left eye socket when she noticed the green glowing serum surging through the tiny veins in the eye. The population of the serum in the eye made the white of her eye glow a florescent green.

She waited her usual time frame watching and observing. The serum was visible this go round. She could see the green run through veins and course through the eyes. She wondered what was making it move so quickly. The corpse does not have a circulatory system to push it through.

As Dr. Miller walked close to the body ready to inject the last bit in the soft pallet she noticed the eyes once more. The eyes began to blink. This time no

SERUM

violent reaction the corpse just blinked. Dr. Miller watched the blinking eyes when the mouth opened on the woman.

"Who..." The woman mustered out while blinking. Then suddenly the blinking stopped. She was able to speak clearer. "Who... are... you..."

Dr. Miller leaned over the face and smiled. I am Dr. Miller. I need to know something before we get too far. Who is Corey?"

The face frowned and looked upset. "Is he ok?" The woman asked. Dr. Miller shook her head yes not knowing one way or the other. "He is a dear sweet boy."

Dr. Miller trying to be quick not knowing if the serum would work for an extended period of time or not. "Who is Corey? You want us to protect him. How do we find him?"

"He is a dear boy..." The corpse was interrupted.

"How do we find him?" Dr. Miller trying to hurry things along.

"Honey do you want to hear the story or not? Who is telling it anyway?" Dr. Miller was surprised at the way the woman spoke so clearly. As Dr. Miller took a step back in amazement the head of the corpse moved to the side never losing sight of the doctor.

Dr. Miller spoke in amazement that the head was able to move. "Take your time." Lacy propped herself against the instrument table and put her hand over her mouth in, awe, that the corpse was more lifelike and more active than others before.

"Like I was saying dear. Corey is in the wrong business. I told him he was out of place. I protected him as much as possible. I kept him away from the gang. I meet him at the bank and bought everything he had so he would never have to go back to the tent city. I even gave Timmy the little gifts Corey would send him. He was just out of place."

"Can you describe him to me? Corey that is." Dr. Miller took her hand from her mouth and moved closer to the corpse watching as she was ab e to give fill facial expressions.

"He is tall and thin. He has dark black hair and beautiful piercing eyes. He said he was just doing this to get some money to adopt a child." The corpse watched as the doctor fell back against the intermer t table. The tools clanked together almost musically.

"Are you okay dear?" The corpse said.

"You just described my friend to a 'T'." Dr. Miller straightened up adjusting her lab coat. She looked shaken. "Why does he need protection?"

"There is a gang of dealers. Corey moved too fast and infringed on their territory. That's when they questioned Timmy and I..." She looked like she had

SERUM

just remembered something terrible. "Did Timmy make it?"

"The boy found with you. No..." Dr. Miller stopped herself from telling the woman that she in fact did not either.

"Damn. Damn... Doc we have to get ahold of Corey and warn him they are out for blood. How long till I'm on my feet again?" The corpse asked.

"Miss what's your name?" Dr. Miller asked.

"I am Maud. I'm sorry I didn't introduce myself." The woman leaned her head up and started to look at the surroundings.

"Maud I am going to run upstairs and get my cell phone. I want to show you a picture of Corey." Lacy watched as she nodded her head. This still amazed the doctor that the serum worked on muscle function in the head so well.

Lacy left the room in a hurry not wanting to be gone long. She was in awe that the drug worked so well but didn't want to chance the fact she might be out like a light at any moment.

She stormed off the elevator into her office across the hall. She grabbed the iPhone from the desk and made it back to the elevator before the doors had closed back. While in the elevator she pulled up Facebook and found a group photo they took on one of their Sunday fun day excursions.

She stormed off the elevator back to the Morgue. She had to swipe the badge a couple time because she was so nervous. When she comes through the doors she dropped her access card. She looked at the autopsy table and the corpse on it. Maud was sitting upright with the white sheet wrapped around her.

When Maud noticed the look on Dr. Millers face she knew the answer to the question she was about to ask. "Doc why am I in the Morgue?"

Lacy picked up her access card and walked slowly toward the table. "Miss I need you lay back down for me."

"I'm not doing a damn thing until I get some answers. Why am I in the morgue? Why can't I feel anything? I don't even think I am breathing." Maud sat on the edge of the table holding the sheet around her.

Lacy moved closer. "You died. I used a serum I designed to reanimate your head and brain to find out who you were and if Corey was my Corey." Dr. Miller held up the iPhone showing Maud the photo.

Maud looked and squinted her eyes, "That's him."

"Shit... Shit... How do I contact him?" Lacy propped up against the table looking at her shoes.

"Honey I don't know. Last we talked he was going to move to another drug. He was moving up quick to get out quick is what he said. Now tell me

SERUM

what the fuck I am supposed to do?" Maud looked irritated and green flashed across her eyes.

Lacy looked at Maud in amazement. She tried to decide how she would go about putting her down. "I need to think for a minute. You should not be able to control this much of your body."

"Well la-de-fucking-da I can. Now what?" Maud tried to stand. She was unable to make her feet move like she wanted them to.

"No don't try to stand lie back down and let me take a look at you." Lacy motioned to the table. Maud did as instructed and laid back down, making sure to keep hold of the sheet.

Lacy fumbled to the interment table looking for an empty syringe. She got what she needed and opened the drawer to find a vial of potassium. She filled the syringe and took a deep breath.

"What's that?" Maud looked at the needle in her hand. "I don't like shots. You are not sticking that thing in me." Maud started shaking her head no.

"Miss you need to let me give you this shot. I need to figure out what is going on here. You told me already you can't feel anything. This won't hurt." Lacy leaned over the body.

"What will it do?" Maud asked.

"This is a high concentration of potassium. It will counter the effects of the serum I used to reanimate your mind, and apparently your body." Lacy said while looking for a good injection site.

"Oh no you don't!" Maud yelled and jumped up from the table. As she lunged up she pushed Dr. Miller causing her to fall on the instrument table striking her temple. Lacy slumped onto the floor unconscious where blood from her new wound began to pool.

5

Corey woke up very abruptly from a bad dream. When he came to the realization that it was real, he forgot the main reason it was a bad dream in the first place. He crawled out of bed and went over to look in the mirror. He looks and stared at his face. He noticed how this job had aged him. He was getting wrinkles around his eyes.

"That's it. After this whole thing is over I will be going by the dentist for a cleaning and filler." He said out loud to himself. He used the term dentist from a joke he had heard from Joan Rivers referring to Botox.

He showered and shaved and got ready for his day. He would do the usual. He would go by the coffee shop and get his usual pour. He would down that while walking to his next new ritual, The Salty

SERUM

Dog. He would eat and drink the stress away and then he would go for his pickup.

After his pickup, he would head uptown and wait on the time to head over to the park. Probably at a nice bar in a nice building next to the park. He thought while showering, how much he had used drinking to help him deal with the stress of this job.

As planned he walked out of the building and went on his way to the coffee shop. He got his large and went on his way to the next stop. The Salty Dog was dead this time. It was a hit or Miss for the traffic in the hole in the wall.

He went for his pickup half-drunk from the bar. He shared the usual Coors Light with Pedro, got his stash and headed up town. Today he wanted to try a new bar. He went to a nice-looking place sandwiched between a hotel and apartments. The sign out front advertised a martini special.

After going inside, he sat at the bar. He wondered how many people sat at this bar with a couple pounds of heroin in their bag. He was greeted by the bar keep. Corey knew he was in an upscale place when the man behind the bar was in a tuxedo.

"Sir, how can I help?" The well-dressed older man asked.

"I noticed a special on martinis. I will have one dirty please. Vodka not gin, if you please." Corey

196

noticed that his proper Cotillion English come out when ordering from a man in a tuxedo.

"Right away sir." The man in the tux sounded snobby. Probably thinking Corey didn't know a thing about how to dress or tip in a place like that. The truth is Corey come from money. He was gay and disinherited. He knew that the "Special" on a martini meant a twenty-dollar drink. He also knew to tip at least half in a place like this.

The man in the tux brought back the neatly made drink and Corey promptly placed forty-dollars on the bar. "Keep the change," Corey said biting into an olive on the straw.

The man in the tux was caught off guard as he noticed the sizable tip. "Why thank you sir." He said changing his tune from snobbish to gracious. "My name is Gerald, if you need anything else."

Corey nodded and proceeded to drink. Gerald kept making him drinks and talking about how he was about to become a grandparent in about a week. He was so proud. Corey only pretended to care. He had his mind set on a child himself. He even considered telling the story to the man making him more drunk. He decided to just sit and listen.

Corey got drunk. This time more drunk than usual. He wondered if he would encounter the thug in the park. As he thought about the possibility he drank more. As the sun began to fade in the distance he

SERUM

shook Gerald's hand and congratulated him on the new grandchild.

Corey left the bar almost stumbling. He walked across the street to the park. It was the height of daytime traffic. He had to weave between cars stuck waiting on the light. Corey entered the park gate and took a deep breath.

He said aloud to himself. "You will catch this man on tape today and be done with this job."

CHAPTER 9

SERUM

Lacy woke up to numerous Missed calls from Detective Cox. She had the phone in her hand and needed to focus on the screen as she sat up. She noticed the time on the phone, eight pm. She raised the other hand to her head feeling the gash.

When she realized what had happened she began to panic. She was in the floor of the morgue. She looked over to see the still full syringe of potassium next to her. the phone rang again. This time she answered.

"Will what's up? I must have fallen asleep." She knew she had been knocked unconscious. She knew how. While waiting on a reply she made it to her feet to see an empty autopsy table. Her already open head began to pound.

"Doc, what the hell?" The voice on the other end was out of breath. "We need you. There has been another murder."

"Text me the address." She hung up the phone abruptly.

Looking around the room she began to piece what happened together. The last thing she remembered is that she was talking to Maud about the syringe contents. She was fully mobile. Then darkness.

She looked in the mirror at her gash in her forehead. It looked to have been cleaned. She felt it and noticed that it had was still fresh. She looked at her lab coat and noticed blood. There was ro sign of blood on her face. There was no blood anywhere besides the lab coat. None on the floor. None anywhere you would expect there to be with a large head wound.

She shifted her focus to the real problem. Maud... Where was she? Did she make it out of the building? She began to look around the room. There was no sign of her. She went out to the ambulance bay to the rear of the main room. The door was still open from someone leaving. The wind whistled as she peered out the door to the lit city background.

She felt a pain. This time not from her head but her stomach. She latched the door and ran to the restroom next to her lab. There she began to heave. The thoughts of what was going to happen to her coursed through her mind. She let the sick feeling pass and moved to the sink to wash up.

There she got a good look at her gash in her temple. It was bad. But where did all the blood go? She knew she had lost a substantial amount by the dark circles under her eyes. She felt the phone buzz in her pocket. The address of the next crime scene.

She had to go to her office and put on some makeup to cover the hellacious look. She went to the elevator and looked at her phone. She had another

SERUM

murder in the park. This was the least of her worries because she also had a Missing walking talking corpse.

'With any luck, the person in the park is Maud.' She thought as she made it to her office. She rambled through her bag looking for a compact. Flipping the concealer open to revel a mirror she took another look at the gash. 'This will need stitches. I will go after I leave the park.'

She put on as much makeup as she could to cover the dark circles and make the gash less noticeable. She headed out to the street to hail a cab. A bright yellow taxi pulled up and she gave the instructions to its driver.

'The body in the park couldn't be Maud. Will would have noticed. Wishful thinking.' She looked out the window thinking nothing more than how much her head hurt.

When the driver dropped her off outside the park she knew where to go. There was flashing blue lights in the distance accompanied by bright halogen spots. She walked on the sidewalk with her shoes clacking. Each clack made her head pound more.

Detective Cox noticed her coming from the distance. He met her at the bright yellow tape line. "What the hell happened to you?"

Lacy replied while walking under the tape line. "I tripped in the autopsy room and hit my head on the side of the table. It's not as bad as it looks." She lied to keep him from worrying, but she knew that it was bad. She could feel the results of massive blood loss. Her head pounded and she needed to get some electrolytes in her. She decided she would go by the nearest hospital before going back to the Morgue.

"Well Doc there is not much to tell you. It looks like the same thing we saw a couple weeks ago. The victim was shot at close range in the chest. No one saw anything. The ID on him was fake. I again suspect drugs. This one was clean looking though." Lacy, walking behind Will while he spoke, was only half listening. She was more concerned about her head.

They came to the public park restroom where the body was laying outside the men's entrance. She instantly felt her heart skip a beat. She grabbed Will by the arm and nearly lost her balance. The body was face down, but she knew. She knew because of the messenger bag she bought him from Prada last year when he got his reporting job. She knew because of the cardigan that had an Indian pattern to it. She knew because she recognized the deceased and everything about him.

"I have to sit down Will. I think I am going to be sick." Lacy slid down the side of the detective and landed on the ground. William yelled at the ME waiting on Lacy. He ran over to see about his boss.

SERUM

Lacy lying on the ground at a crime scene began to weep and sob. Looking up at Detective Cox she said, "What will I tell Mark?"

"Doc, you know this guy?" Will asked causing her to increase the sobbing.

The junior ME said, "Dr. Miller I think I need to get you an ambulance. You look horrible."

She shook her head yes knowing she could not look over the body. She knew she needed to be looked at. She agreed to the ambulance. Before it arrived she had passed out. From the stress, the blood loss, or a combination of the two.

2

Mark was doing his weekly load of laundry when he got the call. The woman on the phone was from Mount Sinai Hospital up town. The woman on the phone said she was told to call him as an emergency contact. Lacy Miller is a patient and being admitted.

Mark threw his sweater on the floor and grabbed his wallet to bolt. He was moving so fast he almost forgot to put back on his jeans and almost left with his pajama pants on.

He flagged a cab from the street and told the driver to rush to the hospital. While in the cab the worst-case things went through his mind. The woman calling him could not give any details over the phone.

Mark was dropped off at the emergency room entrance and ran to the information desk. The woman behind the desk sounded like the one from the phone call but he could not be sure. "Can I help you?" She asked.

"Yes, someone called. My friend, Lacy Miller, has been brought here." Mark's voice sounded panicked.

"We have been expecting you. Please go to that door and I will buzz you back." The woman pointed to a sliding glass door that you could not see through. It had sort of a frosted coating on it.

The receptionist picked up the phone while he was walking to the door. He recalled when his dad had a heart attack and he had to rush to an emergency room much like this one. The feelings and emotions rushed through his mind. 'What if she is dead?' The last time he had to be in a place like this his dad was already dead.

Mark was greeted on the other side of the door by a male nurse. Mark under any other circumstances would have been attracted to him. "Are you Mark?" Mark nodded to the nurse. "This way please."

SERUM

Mark followed diligently behind the nurse and was taken to *Emergency Room C.* When Mark walked in he saw Lacy laying on the table with her eyes closed. Mark said "Thank God. Are you okay?"

Lacy opened her eyes. She looked at Mark and began to sob again. The nurse said, "She has been crying on and off for an hour. We had to give her blood. She has a nice head wound and lost a good bit of blood."

Mark walked over to her and put his hand on her right arm. "What happened baby?"

Through the sobs she managed to say, "I fell." After a moment of more crying she looked at the nurse and said, "Can you give us some privacy please?" The nurse shook his head and walked out of the room closing the door behind him.

Mark looked down at her frowning. He knew not to ask any more questions. She would talk when she got ready. The only thing in Marks mind was that someone raped her. He was on pins and needles waiting on her to speak.

After what felt like hours, only ten-minutes in real time, she cleared her throat and began the story. "I had to use the serum again, Mark." Mark looked away as he knew now what had happened to her head. "I had to... It was for Corey." Mark turned and looked back at her. This time with surprise and not anger.

"What do you mean for Corey?" Mark squeezed her hand in his. "Is the one you were telling me about at the bar? What did you find out?"

"Mark... The serum worked better than I could ever have expected. The woman come alive with less of the serum than I had previously used. She was within a matter of minutes able to move more of her body than just her head. She described Corey exactly. Then I got scared. She was able to sit up. When I tried to administer the drug to stop the brain she pushed me. That's how I got this." She pointed to her head.

"What did she say about Corey? What happened next? Did you get her put out?" Mark was in a nervous panic. His mind was running a thousand miles a second.

"I don't know..." Lacy looked at her hands.

"What the Hell Lacy?" Mark yelled and let go of her hand.

"I woke up on the floor. Sit down Mark please and try to remain calm. I need you here for this next part." She patted the hospital bed. He sat like she instructed. "I woke up on the floor to my phone ringing off the hook. The body gone. The person calling was Detective Cox. He was calling telling me that he had a body in the park." She was fighting back the tears this time. She told herself it was for Mark.

SERUM

Mark just looked emotionless as she started with the next part. "The body in the park was Corey."

Mark just stared blankly at her. No response was given, not even a blink. Mark looked dead himself. His skin began to turn pale as the color left his face. Lacy felt his wrist and pushed the emergency button on her bed. The nurse ran in. "What's wrong?"

"He is in shock. His heart rate is extremely low." As Lacy spoke a doctor came into the room. As the doctor put his hands-on Marks neck to feel for a pulse he jumped.

"What are you doing?" Mark yelled. "What do you mean it was him?"

The doctor looked at Lacy puzzled. She said, "false alarm I guess?" The doctor and the nurse stood next to the bed as he began to breathe heavily. Tears began to stream down from his face. Not sobbing or crying. Mark was full on angry. He stood up and walked out of the room. The doctor and nurse behind him making sure he was going to be okay.

Lacy sat in her bed starting to sob again. She knew Mark was angry. Was it at her or was it at Corey. She thought there could be the third option, he was angry at himself.

Mark walked out of the emergency room and on to the street. He just walked and thought. He thought to himself about letting Corey go on this assignment. He thought of how Lacy was, kind of, supportive. He thought of Lacy and the serum. 'Why the hell did I ever let any of this happen,' he thought.

After an hour or so the nurse come in to tell Lacy they had a room ready for her. She looked up and replied, "I am not staying. I know you gave me blood and all, but I am a doctor and know the signs. I will come right back if I feel any of them. I have some business to attend to and can't do that setting here in this bed."

As the doctor prepared her discharge papers Lacy put her clothes back on. As she was slicing on her last shoe Mark come through the door. "Lacy I have to know what happened. I have to tell the little shit how I feel. You can make that happen. You will make that happen."

Lacy stood up and thought for a minute. "I can't do it, Mark, not to Corey. I know him. It's not like reanimating the faceless people on the street."

"Lacy you don't understand. This is not a request I am making here. I am telling you that you will do this. You owe me. You owe me for everything you have put me through." Mark had one tear stream down his face as he commanded her.

"Let's go back to my office then and talk for a bit about it first." Lacy's doctor brought the paperwork in and handed it over to her. She signed the form saying she was leaving against medical advice.

SERUM

"Come on..." Mark said and walked out of Room C. Once on the street Mark hailed a cab and gave the address of the Morgue ten blocks down. The entire ride was in silence. Both were in their own mind trying to plan out the next move.

Once back at the office Lacy buzzed them both in with her access card. Mark followed her to her office. Once inside she closed the door and opened her bottom desk drawer from which she pulled two Styrofoam coffee cups and a bottle of scotch. "We could both use this," she said while pouring a cup and handing it over to Mark.

"How did he die?" Mark said taking the cup.

Lacy took a large sip and said, "He was shot..." She paused to see if he was going to break down and cry or something.

"You know Lacy. I went through the separation anxiety and all the shit that goes with it. I felt hollow without him. Doing laundry, cooking, watching a movie, all was hard and took time. I have already adjusted to being without him. I was hoping that he would be home on Friday or Saturday. I never thought this adjustment would come in so handy. If he had died while we were living together and spending every hour not at work together, I would be a basket case." Mark held the cup firmly.

"Mark I need you to stay here and let me go downstairs first. I need you to let me make sure he is here. Also, I don't want you seeing him fresh out of a body bag. Let me process him first. I will come back up for you in a bit." Mark shook his head.

"Leave the scotch." Mark said and she nodded.

3

Once in the basement she went to see if Corey had been brought in yet. She walked into the room where she just a few hours ago reanimated Maud, Corey's friend. She walked over to the spot where she woke up and picked up the syringe of potassium. She put it back on the table next to the half full syringe of glowing green serum.

She noticed when Maud took off she had taken the sheet used to cover her. There was no sign a body had even been on the table. Lacy looked around and noticed the toe tag of Maud on the floor. She picked it up and put it in the pocket of her dress.

Lacy walked over and picked up the clip board hanging next to the morgue body cooler. She looked on the list and found, Corey Avery(?), down at the bottom of the page. The ME signed him in just thirty minutes ago. She took note of the drawer he was in.

Dr. Miller went to the table that Maud laid earlier that afternoon. She straitened the tools and

SERUM

made sure she had enough serum in the syringe to complete the task. She thought about using another syringe. She thought, 'He is dead... Why?' She didn't have any of the other strains of serum to inject in him.

She was afraid of what might happen with the green strain. She needed to tell Mark to make it snappy. She doesn't need to risk the total reanimation of Corey. She could only think of where in the fuck Maud was. The serum was not supposed to reanimate the entire corpse.

She, talking to herself while walking to the cooler doors, said, "What is going to happen here? How the hell am I going to fix this?" She opened the door where Corey's body bag lay. She pulled the drawer out and unzipped the bag. Taking a deep breath, she opened the bag to see the face.

It was Corey. He was still in his cardigan all blood stained. Lacy went around the corner to fetch a gurney. Her head began to pound thinking about what she was about to do. She was about to reanimate on of her best friends. Somehow to her it was only morbid because she knew the person. This time she had a rush of morality hit her causing her to stop and think. The same question went through her head. The question that conveniently escaped her when she was experimenting on the bodies in previous days. 'Just because I can, should I?'

She managed to maneuver his bag and body on to the gurney and from the gurney to the autopsy table. She worked the bag off and looked at him. She was about to cry but fought the tears back. I can't cry. I need to stay strong.' She looked him over he had been eating well. He had to have gained a good ten pounds since the last time she had seen him. She noticed the skin beginning to turn grey. The blood in the capillaries was starting to congeal leaving him looking dead.

She wanted to get Mark down here fast so she could begin. So, he could still see him before he started looking more like a corpse. She got a fresh sheet and covered the fully clothed body up. She would have another ME process and do the autopsy tomorrow. She didn't think she could do it on her friend.

Lacy left the room for the elevator leaving Corey behind. She walked back into her office to find Mark with about half a bottle gone of the scotch. "Are you ready to do this?" She asked.

Mark sat the bottle on the corner of her desk and made it to his feet. "Let's go. Lacy and Mark walked silently back to the elevator. On the bottom floor Mark felt an overwhelming emotion come over him. He sat on the ground just outside the lab doors.

"Are you okay?" Lacy asked.

"I will be. He is not going to have a crazy reaction, like before, is he?" Mark just stared down

SERUM

the hall to the double door where he knew his husband lay.

"The woman I used this serum on just woke up. She also is Missing. So, we are going to have to make this quick Mark. Do you understand? I can't risk him gaining full animation. You need to say your goodbyes and let me pump him with as much potassium I can." Mark stood and looked at her. He nodded to let her know he understood.

Mark followed her to the double doors leading to the morgue. With a sigh, he followed her inside. He noticed the sterile smell as he walked in. There on the familiar table was a body under a white sheet. Mark began making a noise. Lacy grasped his hand and rubbed his back. The noise he made was not that of crying. It was a sad noise. Mark wasn't even aware he was making the noise.

Lacy left Mark standing about ten feet from the table and walked over to the corpse of Corey. She looked at Mark and said, "We don't have to do this. You know that right?"

Mark stood silent for a second. "We are doing this Lacy. I am going to have my last words with him. You are going to make that happen."

Lacy nodded and uncovered the top portion of the body revealing the head and upper part of the chest. You could see some of the blood spatter but none of the bullet entry wounds. Mark once again fell silent. He put his hand to his mouth and stood there motionless.

Seeing the body and talking about it are two different things. Mark just found out how different. He was flooded with emotion and memories. He, standing motionless and silent, remembered when he popped the question in front of Lacy. He remembered the time they went to France and he left the camera on the rail of a bridge after the light show on the Eiffel Tower.

Marks thought was broken with Lacy asking, "Are you okay?"

Mark just blinked like he was snapping out of a daydream. "Yeah I am okay. Let's get started. It is getting late." He looked at the clock and said, "Well, early."

Lacy walked around Mark to grab the syringe she used on Maud. Mark stood toward the foot of Corey's body. Lacy leaned the head forward and walked up the spine looking for the right spot to inject the serum. When she found it, she looked over at Mark and nodded. Mark replied with a nod of his own signaling for her to start.

While she injected the serum at the base of the spine. Mark noticed the face of his now deceased partner. The face began to lighten in color. The grey faded back to almost a flesh tone. Then he noticed the

SERUM

green. The glowing green in his neck. He guessed right about the spot the thyroid gland was.

Lacy laid the head back on the table and said, "I want to wait a minute before I do the next injection." Mark again nodded in agreement and watched the face intently. Time seemed to pass slowly, but after five minutes Lacy walked back to the face of the body.

She leaned over the head lifting the right eyelid. She held the syringe just over the eye and looked back at Mark. "You may want to turn your head for this part." He shook his head no and focused on the face as she moved the needle above the soft eye.

She injected half of the small amount she had left. Again, like before the small veins in the eye began to light up with the green glowing liquid. The effect was so pronounced that Mark from the foot of the body noticed.

"Did that happen before?" Mark asked.

"Yes, it did. I will put the rest behind the other eye and none in the soft pallet. The corpse before him didn't need any more than that." Lacy moved around the table so she could get a better angle on the left eye.

When she lifted the lid of the second eye she almost jumped out of her shoes. The pupil cilated. Mark noticed the jump. "What is it Lacy?"

"His pupil dilated. That's quicker than before. Maybe because the body had not been sitting quite as long as the one before." Lacy took a step back and d d not inject the extra amount. Both eyes flung open wide and looked at the celling. They then began to blink.

Lacy looked over at Mark who formed a single tear that was streaming down his right cheek. "How long will this take?" Mark asked.

"It should be quick." She said looking at him wondering if that was a tear of pain, loss, or remorse.

"What should be quick?" A faint voice said that Lacy and Mark knew was not their own. It was the voice of a friend. It was Corey's voice.

Mark and Lacy exchanged a look saying nothing. Mark wiped the tear from his cheek and began to walk to the head of the now talking body. "Hey babe,..." Mark said leaning over Corey's head.

As Mark looked into Corey's eyes he noticed them dilate with green glowing specks in the iris. Once Corey focused on Mark he said, "Mark where are we? Why can't I move?" He began to blink.

Mark looked at Lacy for a second before speaking. She hoped he would take pity on him now that he had seen the reanimation happen. "Where the fuck do you think we are?"

217

SERUM

Corey's face had a startled look on it as Mark peered into his eyes. "Are we in the hospital? Last thing I can remember is that that thug had pointed a gun at me. He was talking about teaching me a lesson." Corey looked as if he were deep in thought. "Did he shoot me? Am I paralyzed? Oh God..."

Mark looked back over to Lacy and waved her over. As she walked up to where Corey's head was her shoes make a clack noise on the floor and Corey's head moved in the direction of the noise. He focused on Lacy. "Lacy you are here too? This must be bad. Just tell me guys. Make it quick."

Mark looked between Lacy and Corey. He finally said, "Your dead Corey. Lacy was called to where your body lay in the park because you got your stupid ass shot." Corey's face showed an expression of horror and disbelief as he heard Mark speak. "You got your ass shot over a job. A stupid fucking job. You selfish bastard."

Corey begins to make noises of sobbing but no tears came for he was indeed dead. Lacy moved over and put her hand on Corey's forehead. She said with a tear coming out of her eye. "It's true babe. You are in the morgue."

Corey reached his hand out from under the sheet toward Mark. Mark took a step back as he did.

Lacy looked panicked and said, "Mark he is gaining more movement faster. We have to hurry this along."

Mark looked back at Corey and took his outstretched hand. "You selfish bastard I had to say goodbye."

Corey interrupted Mark while speak ng. "This is not goodbye. I am not dead. I can feel. I can talk. I am able to move." Corey looked like he was trying to work a muscle to prove his point. "I can't move my legs yet."

Lacy spoke up. "Corey I can assure you that you are dead. I injected you with a serum I made. You need to listen very carefully. I will have to inject you soon to counteract the serum in your system and turn it off. You are not alive you are dead. You will be sent to a funeral home in the morning." Corey's face displayed every emotion from fear, anger, and confusion.

Corey didn't feel dead he felt very much alive. Corey lifted one hand in front of his face. Looking at a vein in his hand. Where blood should have been flowing blue he saw a rush of the green serum. "Lacy, don't do this. You don't have to put me out. Let me live like this."

Lacy took his hand from in front of his face and held it. "Corey listen. Biologically you are dead. Your body has already flipped the kill switch. Your body will continue to decay. There is no fresh hemoglobin in your body to keep systems alive. If I were to leave you

SERUM

like this you would rot. In about another six hours you will begin to smell. I need you two to hurry this up and let me do the right thing here and put you down to rest in peace."

Mark leaned over Corey and said, "You will let her put you to rest. I had to say my peace, or I didn't know if I could go on with it on my mind."

Corey looked at Mark. "What a selfish ass. You woke me up so you could live with yourself. To tell me, I told you so..."

"Basically yes," Mark replied. "You are the selfish one. You are the one who went off on this dangerous Mission against my wishes. So yes."

Corey looked over at Lacy and said, "Put me out Lacy. I can't cry and I can't feel anything. I can't be a walking rotting corpse. Just do it before I lose my nerve. The nerve I can't feel."

Lacy looked at Mark for approval. He nodded his head recognizing it was now or never. Lacy got the syringe from the table filled with potassium and said, "Ok before I do this Corey. I want to say I will always love you and cherish you as a friend." Corey didn't reply but just blinked his eyes. If he were able to produce tears they would be streaming down his face.

Lacy lifted Corey's head. It wasn't as heavy as before because Corey was using some of his own reawakened muscles to aid in the process.

Mark snapped, "Wait." Lacy laid Core's head back down. "I have to say something." Mark took Corey's hand in his and said, "I want you to know something. You will always be the love of my life. I know I could never find another like you." Mark paused as tears began to stream down both cheeks.

Corey let go of his hand and put it on Marks face wiping the tears from the emotions he had been holding back. Lacy took a step back letting the tears flow herself. "Mark," Corey said. "You are free to try. If you can find love you go for it."

"Corey, you will always be in my heart." Marks words were only a comfort to himself as Corey's emotions seemed to fade. Corey took his cold hand off of Mark's warm cheek.

"Let's do it Lacy." Corey said lifting his head. Mark grabbed Corey's hand.

Lacy took her hand and held the crown of his head as she felt for the spot to stick the needle. She plunged the tip between the two vertebras and slowly emptied the syringe. About half way through emptying the syringe she felt the muscles in his neck begin to relax. She tightened her grip as Corey's head fell into her control.

When Lacy had emptied the syringe, she laid his head back on the table. Mark began sobbing uncontrollably. Lacy put down the needle on the table and went to comfort her grieving friend. Lacy embraced Mark as they watched the expression on

SERUM

Corey fade. The eyelids slowly relaxed and the complexion faded back to grey. Corey had been put to rest as quickly as he had been reanimated with Dr. Miller's strange serum.

CHAPTER 10

SERUM

After putting Corey back in the cooler Lacy and Mark went back to Lacy's apartment where they drank an enormous amount of wine and fell asleep spooning in her bed. The two woke the next morning to a Missed phone call from the morgue.

"Mark... Wake up..." Lacy said nudging him. Mark swatted at her and pulled the comforter over his head. "Mark the morgue just called me." Mark threw the sheets off and jumped to a full standing position in one motion.

"What did they say?" Mark asked wide eyed with a crazy bed-head. Lacy shrugged and pressed redial for the number.

The receptionist answered, "Dr. Miller they need you down here. Something is going on."

Lacy put the phone on speaker so that Mark could hear. "What is happening?"

"I was just told to get you as soon as possible. 'There are bodies piling up,' is all another examiner said. Also, the CDC is here from Atlanta." Listening Mark shrugged like, what does that mean.

"Tell them I will be there ASAP." Lacy hung up the phone not letting the receptionist reply.

"Mark get dressed." He was standing in his boxers and white tank top. "You are going with me."

"Shit, Lacy, why is the CDC at your morgue?" Mark said while putting on his sweater from the day before.

Lacy also was putting on over her slip the same dress from the day before. "We will find out when we get there. Hurry..."

The two dressed and sprinted for the door. Each had their own idea about what the problem at the city morgue could be. Lacy of course thought something with one of the two Missing bodies. Mark could think of nothing but Corey escaping, even after the death dose.

The two rode in a cab in silence. Neither expressing their concern for fear it might be true. When the two arrived at the morgue Mark handed the driver a wad of bills not knowing if it was even enough and jotted out the door.

Once inside there were two MEs at the desk with the receptionist. "Dr. Miller," the tall lanky black man said. "We have a situation on our hands."

The other ME, a chunky short white woman said, "Yeah... I have never seen this before. '

"Let's go into my office." Lacy ushered the two MEs and Mark toward her office. Once inside she shut the door and said, "What is it?"

The two MEs exchanged a look and finally the woman answered. "It is like an animal attack, but it isn't. We are not sure what it is."

SERUM

Lacy looked at Mark somewhat relieved. "So this is an animal attack, how many?"

This time the man spoke, "Three."

Lacy looked at Mark thankful that her scenario was not fulfilled. "Let me see the wound and I should be able to narrow down the type of animal." Lacy walked over and opened her door to lead the three to the elevator.

Once in the cold damp basement Lacy let the other two examiners take the lead to the bodies. While following behind all of them Mark asked, "Were there any animals reported Missing from a zoo or something?"

"Not that any of the detectives indicated." The female ME said.

Mark paused behind the three as they come to the all too familiar double doors at the end of the cold damp hall. He hesitated but followed the rest. The memory of the night before fresh in his mind. The fact that Corey was probably still in the cooler. Mark mustered his strength and followed.

There were three bodies and three tables almost filling all the available space in the room. All three were covered in white sheets. The first table they come to the male ME pulled down the sheet to reveal the upper half of the corpse.

The body was that of a white male in his mid-twenties. The neck of the man was badly lacerated with an open gaping wound. It looked like an animal chomped the jugular open.

"Did he bleed out at the scene?" Dr. Miller asked the other two.

The male ME looked at his counterpart and said, "Very little blood was found at the scene. There was minimal spots on the pavement."

Mark wincing as he looked at the body said, "Where was he found?"

This time the female examiner spoke, "He was found next to the dumpster at the restaurant he worked at. We thought at first that he had been killed somewhere else and dumped there but he had been seen gathering the trash to take out minutes before another cook found him."

Lacy looked over to Mark with a concerned look on her face. "So, no blood and he could not have been killed then moved?" Lacy turned to the instrument table and opened the door looking for a magnifying glass. She looked close and noticed something strange around the edges of the opening in the neck. The other two MEs were leaning over to see what they could.

"Guys it looks like a human did this not an animal. See here," Dr. Miller pointed to the part that looked like two front teeth.

SERUM

The female ME nudged her counterpart and said, "See I told you so." She then walked around to the second body on the middle table and uncovered it to the upper chest. "Dr. Miller see here I think we could get a full dental impression out of this one. We would have to piece it together but I think we could get a full set."

Dr. Miller walked around to look at the teeth Marks. "Guys this is a human doing this. Let's see the third." The all walked around to the third body and Dr. Miller pulled back the sheet. She put the magnifying glass up to the gaping hole in the neck of a corpse. "I can't tell so much with this one."

The male ME said, "Before you ask all three were like the first. Minimal blood around the bodies." Dr. Miller looked up from her magnifying glass to glance at Mark.

"Ok guys do the full work up and try to get a dental impression. Put it in the system to see by chance if there is a match. I doubt there will be but we need it on file in case we get any more like this." Dr. Miller motioned to Mark that they were leaving.

The female ME almost giddy said, "Yes Miss." As Dr. Miller was walking to the door she heard her say to the male ME, "We get to work on a biting serial killer."

Dr. Miller paused and said, "Don't jump to ary conclusions. We can't prove that." She then turned and walked out with Mark.

In the hallway Mark asked, "Why were you giving me so many looks in there?"

Whispering she replied. "When I was in the hospital having the transfusion, I had a head wound from being pushed down by Maud." Mark nodded letting her know he remembered. "What I did not tell you is that when I came to there was no blood on the floor or on me. There should have been gobs of it."

"Well where the fuck did it go?" Mark asked.

Lacy just shrugged in return and said, "I don't know, but it sounds awful fucking familiar doesn't it?"

2

Lacy and Mark decided to head to the nearest Starbucks. They both were in need of some coffee and a talk. They needed to talk about Corey and what to do now. They needed time to grieve with each other. After all the two of them shared an unprecedented experience with each other.

After they both got their drinks and breakfast sandwiches they found a cozy little corner to sit and chat. They talked and decided that Corey should be cremated. They also decided that they would donate the funds from his life insurance to the NoH8 campaign.

SERUM

The major topic of conversation was how Lacy would pull some strings with detective Cox and have the case put to rest soon. She also needed to inform him of his real identity. The whole ordeal had already began to take its tole on the two. Other than the fact that they were both grieving the loss of someone close; it was a great talk.

Just as Lacy and Mark had finished up their breakfast Lacy got a call. The number was not one she recognized but she answered anyway. The woman on the other line asked, "Is this Dr. Lacy Miller?"

"Yes it is." Lacy replied.

"Hi, I am Sandra Mills from the New Your City 911 dispatch center." Lacy's heart fell a few inches when the dispatcher said those words. "I am calling because you are listed as the city's emergency contact for the City Morgue."

Lacy's heart fell again. "Yes I am the Chief Medical Examiner."

"I don't mean to a alarm you but we had a 911 call from the morgue. The person on the other end never said anything. We called back and there was no answer. So we were instructed to call you. We are also sending a squad car to meet you outside the building. Can you be there in ten minutes?"

Lacy replied, "Yes of-course. I am on my way."

Lacy hung up the phone and looked at Mark in a panic. "There was a 911 call at the morgue. Now no one is answering the phone."

"Well let's go. What are we waiting for." Mark lead the way to the street and waived down a cab. They were only four blocks away and could have run. The cab seemed faster to them both.

When they pulled up outside the front of the morgue they had beaten the police. Lacy could think of nothing but the worse. She ran inside ignoring the advice of the dispatcher to wait on the police outside.

She and Mark walked into an empty lobby. Nothing out of place and nothing on the desk or table disturbed. The only thing they noticed was the phone at the unoccupied reception desk was off the hook hanging toward the floor.

"Where did she go?" Mark asked.

"I have no idea. I bet she was the one to call 911." Lacy went around the desk and looked under it. There was no one under it. Lacy looked up at Mark and shrugged.

They walked down the hall to Lacy's office. Again nothing unusual Lacy again leared under the desk to see if anyone was under there.

"Hands up!" A loud authoritative voice said, startling both Lacy and Mark. From behind the desk Lacy stood straight up starring in the face of a Smith & Weston police special. Mark had already spun around and put his hands in the air.

SERUM

"I... I... am Dr. Lacy Miller. The 911 dispatch called me. I am the Chief Medical Examiner." Replied Lacy, trying not to move a muscle.

"Miss, you were instructed to wait outside for us." The officer put his gun in his holster and put his hand on the radio and said, "John she is inside."

"Where is everybody?" The officer asked as another cop walked up behind him.

Lacy said, "I have no idea. I just got here myself. I noticed the phone off the hook in the lobby and no receptionist. Other than that, everything is how it should be."

"Let's look around then. You guys stay behind us." The cop told her. She wanted to say so bad how she also had a badge and a gun but thought it not an opportune time.

Lacy and Mark followed the two city beat cops around the first floor of the building. They went from office to office having Lacy unlock doors and use her pass key. The cleared the entire ground floor. One officer went to start on the upper floors and the other went with Lacy and Mark to the basement.

Once in the basement the officer went from room to room clicking on the lights. The first couple of labs were empty and clear. Just before reaching the private lab that Lacy used to develop the serum there was a noise. They heard it come from the restroom.

The officer put his finger to his lips signaling for the other two to be quiet. Lacy and Mark exchanged looks as he opened the door slowly. From inside the dark restroom came a squeal of epic proportion. The squeal was loud enough to make you go temporarily deaf. The officer with his gun drawn jumped as a woman ran from the shadows and embraced him with a gripping hug.

The woman was the receptionist. She looked unharmed and extremely frightened. She said, "Thank god..."

The officer said, "Are you alright Miss? What scared you? Where is everyone?" The woman said nothing and just sobbed as the officer radioed for an ambulance and to let his partner know he found someone.

The officer tried again. "Miss, why were you in the corner of the basement restroom?"

"The dead were walking..." Was what she said sobbing.

The officer looked at Lacy and Mark. Lacy looked at Mark. They both knew it was not entirely impossible. Lacy looked at the officer and said, "We had three strange bite deaths come in this morning. The CDC was called and should be here this afternoon. Other than that we have a death by natural cause and a shooting fatality."

"Show me where you keep them and let's make sure they are all accounted for." The cop was

SERUM

obliged by Lacy throwing up her arm and pointing to the double doors at the end of the hall. The officer walked to the end of the hall and pushed on the door. The door didn't open.

"It's locked." Lacy fished out her access card and swiped it on the pad next to the doors. The officer pushed on the door again with it letting way for him to enter. As soon as he looked through the door he put his hand over his mouth and walked back into the hallway.

"What?" Lacy asked noticing the look when someone wasn't normally around dead bodies.

The officer took a second to hold back his breakfast. "Two..." He held his stomach and looked the opposite direction down the hall. "Two dead bodies in the floor."

Lacy looked at Mark and yelled, "Two... On the floor?" She swiped her badge again and opened the door with Mark behind her. The officer and receptionist remained in the hall.

When Mark and Lacy went in to the main autopsy room it was in disarray. There were indeed two bodies on the floor. Bodies of the two who were left to process the three bodies from the animal or human attack. The three who had been attacked were gone.

Mark looked at the sheets in the floor, the doors to some of the coolers open, all three instrument tables and one autopsy table overturned. Mark looked at Lacy and said. "Did they get the serum too?"

Lacy said, "No I used the last on Corey." They both had forgotten about Corey and looked at the cooler wall. His cooler door was one of the ones that's door was left open. Lacy ran to the door and pulled out the empty tray. She and Mark exchanged looks.

"What the Hell Lacy. I saw you put him out." As Mark was talking the police officer and his partner were outside the door banging to be let in. Lacy let them in so that the investigation of the four Missing corpses could begin.

CHAPTER II

CHRISTOPHER MCDONALD
1 MONTH LATER

A s the snow began to fall along the Canada US border, Brad, a high school senior, started his shift at the local AM/PM gas station. Brad took the job to help get a ring for his girlfriend who was two months pregnant.

Brad sat in the stool behind the cash register and looked at the snow fall. He liked days like these. Because they had been forecasting the first snow for the last week every loaf of bread and gallon of milk were gone from the store and the roads were clear. Days like these he liked to get one of the Playboys from the stand behind the register and carefully open the plastic so he could reseal it.

Just before the impulse to grab a dirty magazine hit, he had a car pull up. It was a yellow taxi that had the Statue of Liberty stamped on the logo. He thought that it was highly unlikely for a yellow taxi from New York City to be here hundreds of miles away. Not only had the distance perplexed him, but the fact that the city had been shut off weeks ago by the US Military and the CDC.

From the car came a person that Brad most defiantly thought was a man. He was tall and lean. He was well bundled. Brad thought over bundled for the light dusting of snow that was expected that night. When Brad heads out around the end of the shift to

SERUM

change the trash can liners he only wears a medium weight company provided AM/PM hoodie.

The well bundled man opened the gas door and placed the nozzle in. He pushed the regular unlettered button and noticed the flashing sign on the readout to please pre-pay.

Brad thought, 'You dip shit, everyone has to pre-pay or use a card these days. Even at the country store.'

The man realizing, he needed to go inside walked to the door. As he walked Brad was sizing him up. After all he was the first customer of his shift. The man come through the door. His skin was pale eyes were piercing black with jet black hair coming from the brim of his toboggan.

The man looked at the kid behind the register lounging in the seat and asked, "Where do you keep your liquor?"

Brad pointed to a doorway that leads to a small ten by ten room. 'Past the restrooms through there."

The man walked into the heavily surveillanced room. Brad could see him from the monitors behind the register looking for his poison. Brad watched as the man sneezed and sprayed, what Brad would later describe as, the plague, all over the bottles. Brad thought 'I won't be straightening those tonight.'

CHRISTOPHER MCDONALD

The man walked to the counter with a pint of Johnny Walker Red. He threw forty dollars on the counter and said, "Put the change on the pump." Brad noticed the hands. They looked cold like there was no heat in the car. They were almost a purple-blue.

Brad asked the stranger in the yellow New York taxi, "Can I see your ID sir?"

The man looked at the cashier with an, are you kidding me, look. He went for his back pocket and pulled out a black leather wallet. He pulled from it a New York driver licenses. Brad took it from him and read, Mark Avery, DOB: 01/31/1985.

"Well you sure are old enough Mr. Avery." As he punched the date in the computer he thought to ask. "Hey, how did, you come about that car? I thought the city was closed off weeks ago"

Mark looked out the window at the yellow New York cab, and then looked back at the boy. "My father is a retired cab driver from New York. It is his car." Brad nodded his head and put the scotch in a brown paper bag.

"Your pump is ready to go Mr. Avery." Brad said handing over the brown bag.

Mark would never get used to the last name Avery. He took it because Corey used it and died with it. Mark wasn't sentimental by any means to the name but he needed to think of one fast for the man at the fake ID place. The ID place was super busy that day with all of the checkpoints going up.

239

SERUM

Mark grabbed the bag off the counter and headed out to pump the little bit of gas he could while in the snow. Since the quarantine gas prices shot sky high. The sign above the pump said today's price fourteen dollars and thirty cents. Mark would ride the car to the next town on that much and do something to round up more money and maybe another car. This one did yell, 'Check me for the virus.'

The yellow taxi pulled out of the station with another thirty or so mile before Mark would abandon it like so many cars along the road that no one could afford to put gas in. Mark turned on the radio and listened to a station playing the *Golden Oldies.* He thought of when he was young ridding in the car with his father listening to the same style music.

Mark thought about what his father would think if he were still alive. He would probably flip his shit to know what Mark had been up to. Not just the Gay thing but the relationship to the center of the whole virus thing. Mark continued to drive until when the yellow Crown Vic started to sputter, just after passing a sign, *Welcome to Emerson City Limits*, he pulled off the road.

Mark got out with his little brown bag and began to walk in the inch or so snow. The crunch of the snow sounded so cool to him. It almost brought him back to being a child making snow angels. He stopped walking long enough to take the top off the scotch bottle and drink.

Once he had gone a good mile he comes to the actual city center. There was an all-night diner in an Air Stream trailer. There was a hotel called The Crown Inn. Mark thought long and hard about what location he would walk to.

There would be more people at the diner than the hotel for sure. After sneezing and wiping his nose on his coat sleeve he walked in the direction of the diner. He drank a huge swig each couple of steps he made. Right before he made it to the steps on the Air Stream he chunked the brown bag with the empty bottle of scotch inside. It hit the snow making a crunch noise.

Just before entering the diner he looked inside to see about six people inside. There was a woman behind the counter in a yellow dress and black apron. Before Mark opened the door he reached into his back waistband for his gun. Well originally it belonged to Lacy. Lacy no longer needed it.

Mark busted through the door and said, "Hands up everyone!" The tone he took showed he was both serious and desperate. Mark pointed the gun at the woman behind the bar and said, "Empty all you pockets and put everything on the counter or... ' He looked at the woman's name tag, "Pam gets it."

The people of the town cared about Pam and wanted to do all they could to help so they started

SERUM

taking wallets and car keys and everything out of their pockets as Mark had asked.

Mark looked at Pam and said, "Empty your cash drawer into a bag and give it to me." Pam did as he asked and then he said, "Put all these people's things in the bag as well." Again, Pam did as instructed. She walked around the bar taking the keys wallets and loose change and put it in the bag.

Mark motioned for the bag and Pam handed it over. He the bolted for the door bag in hand and everyone's belongings to go with it. He looked out at the parking lot looking for the newest car. He spotted a Toyota Prius. It luckily had a push to start system so he didn't have to fish through the bag for keys.

He got in to the car and pressed start. He drove off as fast as the little four cylinder would take him. The people from the diner just looking from the windows. Mark drove off. The car had at least a half a tank. He estimated it would get him two or three hundred miles before stopping.

He didn't have to worry much about police. The quarantine had most of the northern police force at the border of New York. Mark drove without the radio on. He drove just reflecting. He thought about plenty.

He thought about Lacy and how she had this harebrained idea to reanimate dead people. She was stupid. He had tried to talk her out of it. She did it though. His best friend was a genius. She reanimated corpses.

Mark also thought about Corey and the whole drug undercover operation. It all seemed silly to him now in retrospect. If Cory had not done it he would still be dead. The virus would have taken control of him like it had so many.

After two days of sleepless driving and raiding unsuspecting small-town diners and truck stops, Mark found himself in Seattle Washington. Far away from New York. He wanted to start a new life and let the CDC handle what he had left behind.

When he made it to Seattle he found a reasonable hotel. A Super 8. He paid with cash showing his fake New York ID. He told the clerk he could not go back home because of the quarantine. He made it to room two zero two and passed out on the bed.

Mark slept for at least twenty hours. It was a good thing he paid up two days in advance. Mark dreamt of a time back in New York. He was dreaming of Lacy and her death. He recalled so vividly in his dream how she died. She was attacked. That sadly was not what killed her.

After a long day with the CDC and F3I Lacy came home with Mark to her apartment where the reanimated corpse was waiting. In the dream and real life Mark was unable to move when he saw Corey sitting on Lacy's sofa. Corey looked at them both and

243

SERUM

smirked. 'You both would have me die. Well I won't die."

The alarm woke Mark. Someone must have set it before because he didn't turn it on. Mark walked to the mirror to fine a crummy looking man with a tinge to his skin. He thought how it was the same tinge that Lacy had before her heart stopped.

Of course, when Lacy's heart stopped it didn't kill her. Mark looked away from the mirror and flipped the switch on the nearby TV. The channel on was CNN. The topic of conversation of course was the quarantine. Anderson Cooper was interviewing Dr. Sanjay Gupta. He was asking about the quarantine situation and what the CDC is willing to share.

Mark sat on the edge of the bed and watched intently. He watched as Dr. Gupta said, "Anderson this is an unprecedented situation. As we now know the Virus was man made. It is radioactive and reinvents itself quickly. The mutations happen so quick they can't even make a test for it. We know now, Anderson, the virus causes systems in the body to live beyond biological death. What I mean, Anderson, is basically the dead can live with this virus in them."

"What does it do to people who are alive?" Anderson asked.

"Anderson, this is not known at this time. I heard that some doctors treating this, Like Lacy Miller, the one responsible for uncovering it died but didn't...

What I mean, Anderson is that, they continued to live after their heart stopped. Another aspect that they have released is that the deceased needs fresh blood to stay animated, so to speak. It also travels through body fluids like, saliva blood, urine."

Mark looked away from the TV and back to the mirror. He walked back looking at the veins in his face beginning to darken. Mark felt a thud in his chest. He thought at first it was a heart attack. He realized his heart had stopped. Looking down at his hands and the now purple veins, there was a green florescent light coerce though them.

He turned back to the TV to hear Dr. Gupta tell Anderson, "The CDC has made a new term for what we have here. They are calling it Phase II"